Bria

MEANT 4 MORE

Discover the Next Chapter of Your Life

Meant 4 More

Published by Home Church and Home of Hope
In collaboration with Jaquith Creative, jaquithcreative.com

Paperback ISBN 978-1-7778035-0-6
Audiobook ISBN 978-1-7778035-1-3

Cover design by Nacho Huizar, nachohuizar.com
Book layout by Karissa Paterson and Justin Jaquith.

Contact info@homeofhope.ca for more information or to order additional copies. Also available in ebook format.

Printed in Canada
24 23 22 21 1 2 3 4

WHAT OTHERS ARE SAYING

"Brian Thomson wrote **Meant 4 More**, but his life exemplifies living 4 more every day of his life! This book is an amazing example of what is possible when you let God direct your heart to serve others. These stories and real-life accounts will encourage and challenge you to live a life of action to serve the least of these."
—Matthew Barnett, NYT bestselling author, Co-founder of the Dream Center, Los Angeles, CA

"Brian Thomson has served the Lord on the Home Church team for over forty years. He is an outstanding minister of the gospel and has exemplified excellent, faithful leadership. His work on the team extending the influence of the church through the compassion ministry of Home of Hope has helped thousands. The good news of Jesus has changed lives, and great churches are being built in the nations. I highly recommend **Meant 4 More**."
—Mel C. Mullen, Founding Pastor of Home Church

"I have been privileged to watch God at work as the Home of Hope story has unfolded and Home Churches have been planted in many nations. Some of the stories are hard to read, but they are real stories of God rescuing people through His Church. It has been awesome to see so many lives changed by the Gospel. You will be challenged and encouraged as you read this amazing story."
—Heather Mullen, Founding Pastor of Home Church

"**Meant 4 More** is about answering the call that God has for your life and dreaming with your eyes wide open. Whether you are involved in business, church, education, or government, this story will help you create winning principles for your dream to become reality. Enjoy the read, picture yourself in the story, and allow God to open your mind to the great ideas He wants you to embrace, so you can realize the dreams He has for you coming true."
—Dan Peters, President of Mountain Aire Realty

"Pastor Brian Thomson is a modern-day hero. His passion to help the helpless and make a difference in the world has inspired me in my businesses to also step up and want to make a bigger difference! As you read this book, I know you will also be inspired."
—Dan Wiebe, President, Integrity Group of Companies

"**Meant 4 More** is a window into the heart of Brian Thomson, founder of Home of Hope, and into the heart of the ministry happening through Home of Hope in many places of our world. You will read about the people who discovered their "more" as he trained, equipped, and inspired them to be part of the work being done to rescue the perishing. And you will read about those who have been rescued so that they might discover their "more." I know you will be impacted and inspired to greater purpose as you recognize no matter what age you are or what you have already accomplished, you were **Meant 4 More**."
—Melanie Mitchell Epp, author and speaker

"Pastor Brian is a great man of God. He heard God's calling and started an organization called Home of Hope to help desperate children and women. Home of Hope has been a big blessing for ourselves, our Churches (Home Church Rwanda) and even our country of Rwanda. Home of Hope has been helping many vulnerable children with education, food, clothes and shoes. I have seen the children grow up to be great people. I am hoping Pastor Brian's book will be a blessing to many people."
—Fidele Binyonyo, Home Church Rwanda Overseer

"Reading about my dad's past and how it has made him into the man he is today has been very impactful for me. The person you see on stage or in this book is who he is at home. He is a man of integrity and character, and he is a very hard worker. I know that if you read this with an open heart, it will impact you."
—Karissa Paterson, daughter of the author

"You could say that Brian wears his heart on his sleeve, but it's hard to tell because he rolled up his sleeves a long time ago to be the hands and feet of Jesus to this world. He is one of the greatest examples of how to live a life that pursues God's calling in every season and embraces whatever comes his way. Whether you are in a season of change or a dry spell or looking to keep your momentum soaring, the impacting stories in this book will give you limitless inspiration on how and why you were **Meant 4 More**."
—Joy & JD Hornbacher, daughter & son-in-law of the author

TABLE OF CONTENTS

FOREWORD

I'VE KNOWN PASTOR BRIAN THOMSON FOR MY ENTIRE LIFE. He is the most passionate person I've ever met, and his great energy, determination, and enthusiasm are so inspiring.

Yes, he has carried an unwavering passion for God, but he has also always had a passion for helping people find out why they were created and how they can live a life that is **Meant 4 More**. As you read this book, you will learn that this phrase is not just a reflection of the call of God on Brian's life, but a reflection of the influence he has had on countless thousands of people to step into their purpose and calling.

Brian has always had a way to joyfully prompt or even jolt you into something you thought you would never do. And right after you do it, you realize you needed that nudge not only to discover your purpose, but to discover the joy that purpose brings to your life.

I am one of the countless thousands of people who Pastor Brian has influenced profoundly. I can't imagine stepping out and doing some of the things I have done if Brian hadn't encouraged me that I was meant for more.

Some of my first encounters with Pastor Brian's prompting and prodding came when I was a young boy, and he would encourage me to pray or sing out loud in group settings and in youth ministry. Later, in my teens, it was an encouragement to write a song. One song I wrote at his urging has been sung around the world in many different languages, and it started a passion within me to write and record music, which I still love to do. That passion has touched many hearts around the world.

Later, in Bible college, he encouraged me to give my testimony, and later to preach. Twenty-five years later, preaching is something I am blessed to do several times a week. Often, I run into people I have never met who heard me speak in person or online. I have no idea how many people have been eternally impacted because Brian nudged me to step out and speak.

Many times, Brian prodded me into my calling without me even knowing it. That just might happen to you if you catch the spirit on Brian's life while reading these pages. Maybe your calling isn't to write songs or to speak from a pulpit. Your call might have to do with business, sports, science, or something no one has ever accomplished. Sometimes we need a jumpstart from someone like Pastor Brian, who can encourage us into the "more" we are to live in.

In the last several years, Pastor Brian's passion has turned into a compassion ministry you will read about called Home of Hope. Through this ministry, thousands of children and families, and even entire communities, have been helped, all because Brian saw a need and rallied others with a passion for meeting that need. My wife Becca and I have been so blessed to be a part of this organization for over ten years, and we have seen firsthand the effects of this incredible ministry.

As you read **Meant 4 More**, my prayer for you is that the pages you turn would turn your heart toward what you are meant to be and meant to do. May your heart and mind be opened, and may you be prodded into a future bigger than you could have imagined and with influence greater than you could have dreamed.

Jachin Mullen
Lead Pastor, Home Church

1. IT STARTED WITH 4

Kigali, Rwanda

In December 2006, four children changed my life forever. I was in Kigali, the capital city of Rwanda, with a friend of mine, Elroy Pankratz. A local pastor took us to visit four siblings whose father had died of AIDS two weeks earlier and whose mother was hospitalized with the same illness and was expected by her doctors to die within days.

I peered into the dark mud hut and saw four children with such sad eyes, all huddled together. They looked so hopeless. They had no food and no idea what they were going to do next. I immediately felt my heart break, and I committed to sponsoring them. The next day, the pastor took me to the hospital, and we prayed for their mom.

The sadness in those kids' eyes that day is an image I can never forget. I don't want to forget it. They were mere children, and their desperation awoke something inside me. They weren't nameless faces on a television screen. I couldn't change the channel and pretend they weren't there. I couldn't forget about them and go back to life as usual.

I wanted to do something.

On the flight home, the stirring in my heart was impossible to ignore. God was doing something inside of me. I was forty-eight years old, but it felt like my life calling was just coming into focus. As I thought of those four faces staring up at me and others I had met as well, I knew I was not doing all that God had called me to do. God had made me for more.

I began to weep as that truth sank in. It was the first time I had cried in years, I think. So, there I was, seated next to strangers, thirty-five thousand feet in the air, with tears flowing uncontrollably down my face. I felt like God was rewiring my heart. He was preparing me for a change that was about to take place. Even if I had wanted to, there was no way I could ignore what was happening to me.

That trip to Rwanda began an entirely new chapter of my life. It was a chapter I did not see coming, and it is still being written today. Soon after returning home to Red Deer, Alberta, Canada, I started a ministry named Home of Hope with one mission in mind: to bring hope to as many desperate children as possible.

The last decade and a half have been completely different than I ever could have imagined. I had no idea the places I would go, the things I would feel, or the changes I would be a part of. I couldn't have foreseen the transformation that would take place within my heart and the new level of purpose and fulfillment I would experience. I could not have known the extent to which God would use our team as we answered the cry of some of the neediest, most vulnerable people in the world.

Most importantly, I had no idea how many incredible people I would meet along the way. The story of Home of Hope is not my story, nor is it the story of one organization or one church. It is the story of countless heroes, starting with the children, the mothers, and the community leaders on the ground, as well as the everyday heroes from all over the world who have given their time, money, and prayers toward serving people in need. This is the story of individuals who have decided to live on mission, who were willing to step up and step out, and who accepted God's call to make a difference in their world.

Big or small, we all have a part to play. We were all **Meant 4 More.**

Those four children were meant for more. I was meant for more. You were meant for more. That is the message of this book, and it is the message I believe the Holy Spirit wants to speak into our minds and hearts every day.

> GOD CREATED EACH OF US WITH A UNIQUE BLEND OF TALENTS AND GIFTINGS THAT WILL ONLY BE FULFILLED WHEN WE WALK IN HIS DESTINY FOR US.

In the following pages, I hope the pivotal, unexpected moments of my journey will encourage you to be ready for your own mission field. I hope to inspire you to follow God's call for you. He created each of us with a unique blend of talents and giftings that will only be fulfilled when we walk in His destiny for us.

Along the way, you might laugh and smile as you read some of the stories, and you will likely find tears in your eyes and pain in your soul as you read others. Remember, rather than focusing on what we *can't* do, focus on what we *can* do. We can extend love, mercy, and hope. We can help people, and we can encourage other people to help people as well. We can respond to God as He leads us toward our calling and purpose.

As we begin, I would like to highlight several things. First, as I mentioned above, this is not a book about Brian Thomson, nor is it a book about Canada or Home Church or any of our Canadian pastors and team. Yes, by the grace of God we have played a role, but I am convinced that helping those in need is not about people with more resources or privilege "saving" anybody, but rather about all of us working together to fulfill God's original intent for humanity: to be one people, one family around the world, united in love, with each of us contributing our part. I have received more than I could ever give back. I am overwhelmed with gratitude and awe toward the people in each nation who are serving those around them with a level of grace and faith that never ceases to inspire me.

In our ministry, we are careful not to be the heroes or saviors. We point people to Jesus and Biblical principles. We train and empower local people to find their own solutions and to be a resource in their communities and countries. We focus on education and job creation to give people dignity, confidence, and self-respect and to help break cycles of poverty and oppression.

Second, we are committed to preserving the dignity and integrity of the people whose stories are shared throughout this book. All names and pictures have been used with permission, and stories of specific children have been used with the permission of their parents or legal guardians. We have consulted throughout the writing process with the local teams where Home of Hope is serving. The people mentioned in this book are not victims or statistics, but friends. They are known and loved by our team.

THE PEOPLE MENTIONED IN THIS BOOK ARE NOT VICTIMS OR STATISTICS, BUT FRIENDS.

Third, this book includes stories from many years across several different nations. Africa and Asia are diverse, beautiful continents with dozens of nations and hundreds of cultures, and these stories are not necessarily representative of the countries where they occurred. In many cases, local and national governments have worked hard to address the issues we faced in those early years, particularly in slum areas. We often work directly with local authorities, and we applaud their efforts.

Fourth, reader discretion is advised. While many details have been omitted, what we did choose to include is often difficult to read. We have seen many sad, tragic, and appalling things over the years. Our hearts have grieved many times. We feel it is important to recognize the needs that exist while also looking toward the hope and redemption that God wants to accomplish through each of us. We have tried to include content warnings in the appropriate places, and we ask you to use your discretion as you read, especially if topics of abuse or abandonment could be a trigger due to past trauma in your own life.

Finally, all proceeds from the sales of this book will be donated to the ongoing social outreach work of Home of Hope. If you would like to learn more or contribute directly to one or more of the social outreach projects mentioned in this book, please visit www.homeofhope.ca, or contact us at info@homeofhope.ca.

The four siblings we met in Rwanda, December 2006. From left to right, Emmanuel, Josiane, Marie Claire, and Eric.

2. PREACHING TO THE PIGS

Alberta, Canada

THAT PIVOTAL ENCOUNTER IN A MUD HUT IN RWANDA was my first time visiting the country, although I had been to the continent of Africa twice before. I had seen difficult situations and desperate children in other nations, and I had felt my heart break: both for them and for the enormity of the problems caused by poverty and injustice.

But somehow, this was different. Something was happening. Something I didn't expect or ask for. Something that only God could have orchestrated.

I'd like to share a little bit of my story because, in retrospect, God had been preparing me for this my whole life.

As a child, my family lived on a farm in Alberta. I always believed in a Divine Creator of some sort, but it wasn't until I was sixteen years old that Jesus became real to me. My sister Dian was the first one in our family to give her heart to Jesus. She had an encounter with Him that was so real that it made me want what she had. I asked Jesus to come into my life, and I prayed that whatever He had done in Dian, He would also do in me.

At that moment, everything clicked. Jesus was real. I just knew it. And He had died on the cross for my sins.

A couple of years later, a guest minister visited our church.

He was praying for people at the end of his message, and suddenly he said to me, "I feel like God is telling me that you are called to be a preacher!" He had never met me before, and I was surprised by what he said. He continued, "I believe you will become a youth pastor, and you will have the gifts of the Holy Spirit come on you, and you will love praying for the sick. You will travel around the world for Jesus." He went on and on, sharing things he sensed that God was telling him about my calling and my future, even dozens of years ahead.

I had never experienced anything like it! It influenced my life so much. I assumed I would be a farmer like my dad. The idea of ministry was an entirely new concept to me. To be honest, I always thought church was boring, and I didn't even want to go. Plus, I didn't like public speaking at all. I was so shy that I could hardly stand up in front of my class at school to give speeches or reports.

That prophecy encouraged me to believe that I could become a preacher. Jesus had become so real to me, and I wanted other people to come to know Him as I had. Being a minister would be a way of sharing what I had found with other people. That was the first time I realized I was **Meant 4 More**. It excited me, but I knew I had a lot to learn about preaching.

JESUS HAD BECOME SO REAL TO ME, AND I WANTED OTHER PEOPLE TO COME TO KNOW HIM AS I HAD.

So, I started with the pigs on our farm. There were 400 of them, and I would preach to them. I would shout, "Hey pigs! The Bible says that we are to preach the Gospel to every creature. You pigs are creatures, so listen to what I am telling you from the Bible."

Pigs are easily distracted. It was hard to keep their attention. They would go back to eating, so I'd make a loud noise to get them to look at me again. I worked in the barnyard every day, so I practiced a lot: sometimes to small groups of pigs in a pen, sometimes to all 400 at once. I learned a lot from those pig sermons!

After high school, I went to Bible college for three years. At the age of twenty, I became a youth pastor and got married. Things were happening quickly!

Comfortable Is Overrated

For the next sixteen years, I served as a pastor at Home Church (at the time named Word of Life Centre). I went from working as a youth pastor to pastoring one of our Home Church locations. Then, I became the associate pastor in our Red Deer location, which is the main campus.

Around that time, I did a thorough study of healing in the Bible, and I started to pray for sick people. I began to see healings and miracles, just as the minister had said years before.

One day, I was going to be driving through the city where that minister lived. I called him up and offered to take him for lunch to express my gratitude for his influence on my life. As we were eating, he looked at me across the table with his piercing eyes and said, "Brian, I want to share something else I believe God is saying to you. An opportunity is coming. I see change happening in your life. You need to fast and pray and be ready to know God's will clearly when it comes."

I thanked him, but I told him I was feeling content, I was comfortable, and everything was going great. I wasn't looking for any major changes.

He replied, "Just spend time with the Lord and do what He wants you to do."

When I got home, I shared his words with my wife and my pastor, and I began praying. Soon after that, God spoke to me through another guest minister in one of our church meetings. He was someone I had never met before. He felt inspired to tell me that I should consider traveling and speaking in churches all over Canada and other nations. I was surprised by the idea since I never thought about doing that.

I discussed the idea with my pastor. Over the following weeks, we came to the conclusion that this was the will of God, and four months later, I was sent out with his full blessing.

For the next few years, I had the privilege of speaking in hundreds of churches in over sixty denominations in Canada and many other nations, including the United States, Kazakhstan, Kyrgyzstan, India, Kenya, Mexico, China, England, Japan, the Philippines, and Korea.. It was so fulfilling to be in the center of God's will, seeing people coming to Jesus, watching miracles take place, and starting churches.

They were wonderful years filled with many blessings, but God wasn't done with me. He was just getting started.

In April 2006, at our yearly church conference, one of the speakers called me up on stage and said, "As I look at you, Brian, I see a map of Africa. And on this map, I see churches all over Africa. I also see you taking in gifts for orphans and helping children. God will open a door for you in Rwanda!"

God seems to like surprising us. I think He must get a kick out of watching our faces when we try to process the impossible but inspiring ideas He drops in our hearts.

I wasn't looking for more trips or new ministries. I was busy, and I enjoyed what I was doing. Now, out of the blue, God had dropped a new challenge into my life.

But this time, I didn't want to go.

I Didn't Want to Go

On my previous trips to Kenya, I had seen many poor people. I had felt frustrated that I didn't have the means to help them. To be honest, I didn't want to go back. It is hard to see poverty. It's difficult enough to hear statistics, but it's far more heart-wrenching to look people in the face and feel that you are powerless to help.

Visiting Rwanda with the goal of helping orphans and children was not an easy decision for me, but God worked in my heart. He replaced my fear and doubt with a love for people and a belief that somehow God could use me to make a difference in their lives.

> WE MUST CONTINUALLY BE OPEN TO GOD'S EVER-UNFOLDING PLAN FOR OUR LIVES.

I realized—and this is something I still remind myself of regularly—that I should be careful not to get too comfortable in one place. All of us should be aware of that because we are all **Meant 4 More**. We must continually be open to God's ever-unfolding plan for our lives. When I was a shy farm boy shouting my sermons at distracted pigs, I could never have imagined that one day I would travel the world, preaching and serving beautiful people in some of the most remote areas of the world. I wouldn't trade it for anything. But it meant leaving my comfort zone. Not just once, either, but time after time. So, I began to make plans to go to Rwanda. I was still unsure what I could do to help children or what God might have in store for me, but I wanted to follow His will, wherever that took me.

I knew that if I was going to build some sort of ministry focused on helping children, I should start planning for that now. And the first thing I needed was a name. I immediately thought of Pastors Bob and Katherine Hoover, who had been mentors to me ever since I was a young Bible college student.

Back in the 1990s, every time I was with Bob and Katherine or heard them speak, they would tell stories of their ministry helping orphans in India at an orphanage named "Boys Home of Hope." They invited me many times to join them on a trip, and I finally went with them in 1999. I was amazed by the unique, colorful, friendly country. I remember eating delicious Indian food with some of the boys in the orphanage. They showed me their favorite "technique" for eating food—with their fingers. I asked, "Why don't you use a fork?"

They replied, laughing, "God gave us forks. They are called fingers. The food tastes better when you eat it this way!"

So I tried it, and they were right!

The nearby village suffered from great poverty, but the orphanage was like an oasis. There were tall coconut palm trees and flowers everywhere. On that trip, I started sponsoring a little boy who touched my heart.

Later, after I had begun traveling and preaching around the world, Bob once asked me if I would consider becoming the overseer of the Boys Home of Hope because he was getting older. I replied, "I'm sorry, I am too busy with my preaching and church-planting work." At the time, I couldn't see myself overseeing a home for children. Little did I know!

In 2004, Bob passed away. His wife continued to minister in Boys Home of Hope. I will never forget Bob and Katherine's incredible compassion and generosity, nor the warm, hope-filled atmosphere of the orphanage in India.

After God called me to serve children in Rwanda and other nations, *Home of Hope* seemed like the perfect name. I contacted Katherine and asked if she would allow me to use that name for the ministry of helping children in Africa. With tears in her eyes, she said, "Of course! Bob would have loved that so much!"

Now I had plane tickets to Rwanda and a name for the ministry. But I still had no idea what to expect.

3. WHEN EVERYTHING CHANGED

Kigali, Rwanda

LEADING UP TO THE TRIP TO RWANDA, I had done a lot of research on the country. I had never been very good at paying attention to international news, so I had never heard of the Rwandan genocide. Someone suggested that I should watch the movie *Hotel Rwanda*. What an incredible shock that was! The movie explained in vivid detail the terrible genocide of 1994, when more than one million Tutsi were killed in 100 days. In my research, I learned that due to the genocide and HIV/AIDS, Rwanda had a great need for orphan care and had one of the highest rates in the world of households with children raising children.

I was scheduled to speak first at a conference organized by the largest church in Kigali. After the conference, I preached at another church in the city. When the service there was over, I asked the pastor if he knew of any children in desperate need. He looked at me like we were crazy because there were children in need everywhere!

On that first trip in 2006, we saw the pain of a nation working hard to recover. We also saw, firsthand, countless children and teens who were in desperate, hopeless situations. We worked hard on that trip, supporting local pastors and doing what we could to encourage those we met. But it felt like so little in the face of so much suffering.

I still remember the look in the eyes of the oldest of those four siblings who would become the catalyst for God's work in my heart. She was fifteen years old, and she knew she had to be the caregiver, the mother, for her younger siblings. She was in charge—but she didn't have a clue what to do.

We did what we could to help. We bought bags of food for them. We took pictures of them to share with people back home to raise awareness of the need. Later, I personally sponsored all four of them every month, and I kept in touch with the pastor who introduced us to the kids. I found out later that a few days after we left Rwanda, the children's mother miraculously began to improve, and soon she was released from the hospital. She helped support her family for another nine years before passing away from an unrelated illness.

Love and Tears

As we returned home from Rwanda, all I could think about were those four kids and countless others we had seen. I could feel their hopelessness and desperation, but I didn't know what to do about it.

On our flight home, I started to chat with the woman sitting beside me. It was regular small talk until she asked me what we were doing in Rwanda. I started telling her about how we met many orphans and how we were trying to come up with ways to help them. I didn't make it very far before I started choking up.

The problem is, I can't talk when I cry. Some people can weep and talk simultaneously, and it's always so moving and eloquent. Not me. When I get emotional, I can hardly get an intelligible word out.

I tried to tell her more about our trip, but my eyes continued to well up with tears. Finally, I managed to say, "Wow, I don't know what is happening to me. I didn't cry at all during the entire two-week trip seeing orphans and hearing sad stories."

I gathered myself and tried again. "It was such an impacting trip. We met these four children whose dad had just died of HIV/AIDS, and their mother was on the verge of death, in the hospital with the same sickness. Those four innocent kids, sitting in their mud hut, looked so hopeless, so helpless. I will never forget the sadness in their eyes!"

That's all I could get through. The images of the children we met flashed through my mind with such force and emotion that I had to stop. I choked out the word "Sorry" to the woman next to me, and then I asked Elroy if we could trade seats so that he could tell her about our trip. He moved over and continued telling stories of other children we had met and how we had begun to help. As I listened to him tell more stories, the flow of tears continued.

I cried harder on that flight than I can ever remember crying. I tried as hard as I could to suppress my emotions so I wouldn't disturb the people around me. The flight attendants were concerned and asked if I was okay. I said I was, but I needed extra tissues.

I wept off and on during the entire nine-hour flight from Rwanda to the next layover. On the next flight, which was the final leg home, I tried to sleep a bit, but I continued to cry. What was happening to me?

Maybe you've seen ads online or on TV asking you to give money for suffering children around the world. Often the images are heartbreaking, with clear signs of poverty and malnutrition. But it's so easy just to change the channel. Prior to my trip, that is what I would do. I was the kind of person who would selfishly turn the channel to something less painful and more entertaining.

But when you see a desperate child right in front of you, all selfishness vanishes. There is no remote control; there is no option to ignore. When I saw the most desperate children I had ever seen in my life with my own eyes, everything was different.

Between my memories and tears, God brought a verse to my mind. "God has not given us the spirit of fear, but of power, and love and a sound mind" (2 Timothy 1:7 NKJV).

I had always thought about that scripture in reference to living free from fear, but I had never really focused on the word love. I realized God had begun a deeper work in my life by giving me a spirit of love. That is what was happening to me. It was not just seeing poor children and feeling empathy for them. I was beginning to feel the love Jesus had for those children.

> WHEN YOU SEE A DESPERATE CHILD RIGHT IN FRONT OF YOU, ALL SELFISHNESS VANISHES.

As that realization flooded over my heart in waves, I cried again, and again, and again. It felt like God was operating on my heart. I pulled out a pen, paper, and my Bible, and I began to pray about the things that were racing through my mind.

"Lord, what are you doing to me?" I asked. Verses kept coming to me, and I started to make more sense of what was happening. I remembered Romans 5:5, "For we know how dearly God loves us, because he has given us the Holy Spirit to fill our hearts with His love" (NLT).

God was filling me up with His love. I could never boast that I was the one who naturally cared for these desperate kids. I proved that back when I had changed the TV channel so many times. But God's love for them was as irresistible as it was transformative.

God poured His love into my heart. And I've never been the same since.

Elroy Pankratz in Rwanda, around 2010.

Compelled by Love

"How was your trip, Brian? Tell me about it!"

For weeks, maybe months, after I returned home, those questions from curious family and friends brought immediate tears. I would cry every day. It was ridiculous! My friends and family didn't know how to respond to me. It was so out of character for the Brian they had always known.

People would say, "Wow, you must have had quite a trip! Why are you crying so much?" And, talking through my tears—which, as I said before, just doesn't work for me—I would do my best to answer them.

Besides the emotions, something else began to happen. From that day on, every time I read the Bible, I saw verses about caring for the poor. There are hundreds of them throughout both the Old and New Testaments.

I noticed more than ever how much Jesus loved people and how He was moved with compassion for them. His deep love for people caused Him to do something to help the poor, the sick, the forgotten, the oppressed, the desperate. He loved them, so He served them. For example, Matthew writes, "When He saw the crowds, He had compassion on them, because they were harassed and helpless, like sheep without a shepherd" (Matthew 9:36 NIV).

From the depths of His spirit, Jesus felt God's love for the oppressed people who were hurting and hungry. That true love compelled Him to do something to help. Love is not just feeling pity and walking away. Love moved Him to do something about the needs He saw.

The apostle Paul described it this way: "Christ's love compels us" (2 Corinthians 5:14 NIV). God's love inside me was stirring me, pushing me, compelling me to do something. After that trip, I could never go back to the way things were before, no matter how comfortable I had been. The love of God compelled me to help orphans and others in need.

Home of Hope

I began searching for strategies for putting this love in my heart into action to help more children like the ones I had met in Rwanda. For decades, I had been a preacher, teacher, and church planter; but ministering to children was an entirely new direction for me. I never thought that I would lead an outreach program to help orphans and the poor, and I certainly could never have imagined it would grow into what it is today.

The Home of Hope ministry is part of Home Church, based in Red Deer, Alberta. When we began, the church was led by Pastor Mel Mullen, who has been my pastor for over forty years. From the very beginning, Pastor Mel and Home Church were fully on board with the vision to serve children in need. Today, the church is pastored by Jachin Mullen, Pastor Mel's son. Home Church continues to oversee and guide our relief efforts worldwide. Along with the relief work we have also planted many churches around the world, which I'll describe later on.

In those early days, though, I had no idea what was coming. All I knew was that God had told me to go, so I chose to obey. He had arranged it all. I was one link in His plan to help those children He loved so much. There are many other links, and I am so grateful they have each chosen to respond to God's call to do more with their lives.

Remember, I was forty-eight years old when God revealed another chapter of His purpose for my life. According to my kids, that is quite old (although I disagree). Here's my question for you, though, regardless of your age or geographical location: what is the "more" that God has for you? Are you willing to listen to His leading—even if it means stepping out of your comfort zone—in order to help those He has put in your path? It has often been said that you don't have to cross oceans to help people; sometimes you just have to cross the street.

If you listen to love, you'll find yourself moved with compassion and compelled by God's love.

And that's when everything will change.

4. IT'S FOR THE CHILDREN

Jabana, Rwanda

Throughout the years, we have always looked for creative ways to build awareness and raise funds for children. One fundraiser event stands out in my mind. We rented a dunk tank and had people volunteer to perch on a seat, dangling over the water, while other people threw baseballs at a target attached to a lever that would dump the volunteer into the tank full of water. To make it a little more "fun and exciting," we dumped bags of ice into the water.

I was the emcee, conveniently, and I had a great time convincing people to volunteer or give. I would shout out, "Who wants to sponsor an orphan? Who wants to dunk Pastor Jachin in this cold, icy water? Step right up! Buy three baseballs and throw them at the target. Remember, it's for the children!"

The event took off, and people started laughing and having so much fun. Then someone donated a significant amount to put *me* in the dunk tank, seated over the icy water! I hesitated, and that's when my words came back to haunt me. "Come on, Pastor Brian," everyone yelled. "Remember: *it's for the children*!"

I couldn't resist. And believe me, that water was *cold*! From that day onward, "It's for the children" has been a slogan we often use.

I enjoy stirring others to action. I am a motivator at heart. If I am at an event and the person on stage is asking for a volunteer, I love to get whoever is with me up on stage. I won't go myself, of course—I just want to see someone I know up there. It's more fun that way.

My family says that I push them out of their comfort zones, and it's true. I'll come up with ridiculous dares, like trying to convince our grandchildren to roll in the cold snow in their bathing suits and then jump back into the hot tub. If they don't accept the dare right away, I will start offering candy or some other incentive until I talk them into it. The only person who doesn't fall for my tactics is my wife, Connie. She knows all my tricks.

On a more spiritual level, I try my best to motivate anyone and everyone to follow God's plan for their lives. I've encouraged many people to give their lives to Jesus and have invited countless others to visit our church. I love to motivate Christians to overcome fear and share their faith in Jesus with others. It is exciting for me to stir people to act in positive ways. As Paul wrote to the Corinthian believers, "...your enthusiasm has stirred most of them to action" (2 Corinthians 9:2b NIV).

I'm used to convincing people with my words, but when I returned from Rwanda, something was different. It wasn't just my words, but rather my *heart* that seemed to convince people. My tears of compassion stirred them to action. I didn't set out to do all the things we have done, and I can't explain how it all happened. I just know God changed my heart, and that change began to affect and motivate people around me. My testimony of going to Rwanda and my efforts to sponsor children resonated with people who heard me share. The change in my life and the spirit of love that God had given me spilled out on others, and they became motivated to help.

> LOVE IS CONTAGIOUS. WHEN WE RECEIVE GOD'S LOVE, WE CAN'T HELP BUT SHARE IT.

I didn't have to talk anyone into it. There were no incentives involved, no candy, no silly dares—just people who caught the vision that they, too, are **Meant 4 More.**

Kristi Fisher, a long-time friend of mine, had this to say about the transformation she witnessed in me.

> **KRISTI:** *I watched a man change in front of my eyes. I distinctly remember Pastor Brian as a matter-of-fact preacher who taught with humor and joy. Brian transformed into a man with deep empathy and compassion, and it showed through the constant stream of tears rolling down his face. What could so drastically have captured his heart and transformed him? God had forever changed him—it was the only explanation. It was amazing for me to witness the unfolding of the extraordinary calling on his life.*

I certainly can't take any credit for the change in me or for the effect it had on others. It wasn't me. It was God, and it was love.

Love is contagious. When we receive God's love, we can't help but share it. And when we share His love, we inspire others to do the same. True love is unstoppable and uncontainable. And if we let it, it will change the world.

It Began in Jabana

Four months after my first trip to Rwanda, in April 2007, I went back with a team. I asked for an appointment with the mayor of Kigali, and she agreed to see me. I explained what had been happening and told her we wanted to plant a church that would help the children in the community around it. I asked her what area had the greatest need for taking care of children but did not have a Christian church.

The mayor was delighted to hear my story, and she wanted

to help us. The next day, a couple of men from her office led us on a thirty-minute drive out of the capital city of Kigali up a steep, bumpy dirt road to a needy area called Jabana. The local leaders introduced us to the children with the greatest need. With permission, we took their pictures and wrote down their stories.

We held an outdoor church meeting, and nearly one thousand people attended! When we gave an invitation for salvation, they all raised their hands. That Sunday, we started a church there with about four hundred people. In Jabana, there were no buildings to rent, and only small mud huts for homes, so we met under the biggest grove of trees we could find. A man from Kigali whom we had met on our trip in December became the pastor, and I agreed to raise sponsorships for twenty children as part of the work.

And just like that, we planted our first church and launched our first ongoing relief program for children in need.

Generous people back home in Canada began asking how they could sponsor kids as well. Someone volunteered to design sponsor cards. I remember putting the sponsor cards of the four kids that I had met in Rwanda on our refrigerator so that I could see them throughout the day. When visitors would come over to our house, they'd ask me about my trip. Of course, I'd start choking up, unable to talk, so I'd take the sponsor cards off our refrigerator and show them. Several times, visitors *kept* those cards because they wanted to sponsor one of the kids! I finally had to hide the card of the one child left, Emmanuel, because I personally wanted to continue sponsoring him.

I was amazed at people's response, and I asked our contact in Rwanda to send pictures of twenty more children in need of financial assistance. He sent me their names and photographs. Many of them were orphans. We made sponsor cards with each child's story and picture. At the time, I was frequently invited to travel and speak in churches across Canada. When pastors called to invite me, I would ask if they would allow me to share briefly about the new project that

I had started. They always agreed and encouraged me to talk about Home of Hope for a few minutes before beginning to preach.

After the services, I would always be surrounded at the back table where the sponsor cards were. I remember one service where forty children were sponsored! Many people became sponsors, both in our Home Church locations in Alberta and at the places I spoke at all over Canada.

I fell in love with the Rwandan people in the rural area of Jabana. The people had few material possessions at the time, but they love life, and they enjoy dancing, singing, and sharing what they have with guests. I enjoy visiting so much. Rwanda has a particular kind of small but delicious banana, and I tell my Jabana friends, "I love Jabana and I love bananas!" They always laugh at me. It is an honor to partner with them to serve children and mothers in need.

Kristi, who I mentioned earlier, visited Jabana with a team I took over in April 2007. Here is what stood out to her.

> **KRISTI:** *Going to Rwanda was a very pivotal experience in my life. I saw the hardest things. It was my first time to see poverty in front of my face, in its reality. You think you know poverty, but you don't until you are standing in it. You can't know the pain of a mother by looking at a television screen. It's not real until you are standing beside her, breathing the same air.*
>
> *Our team traveled on a very bad mountain road (Rwanda is known as the "Land of a Thousand Hills") to a place called Jabana, a rural area with children everywhere. I found out that none of them had ever seen white skin before! Some kids screamed in fear when they saw our white faces. We asked our interpreter, "Why are they so scared? What are they saying?"*
>
> *He replied, "The kids are saying, 'Mom! What happened to their faces?'"*

Many had such desperate needs. I saw five-year-olds holding infants. Children were caring for children, babies caring for babies. They all seemed to have only one set of clothes (usually with holes), and they had little food, some only eating small portions of rice maybe once a week.

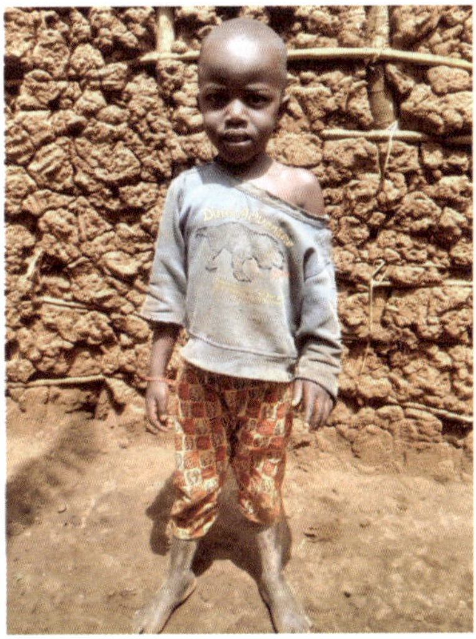

With a translator and a notebook, we interviewed children to find and help the most disadvantaged kids. "This child does not have parents. This child has no food in their home at all. This child has nothing." I was used to interviewing people for jobs and assessing their level of intellect and social awareness. I was not used to interviewing kids about what level of hunger they were experiencing or how desperate or isolated they were, or how many children they were caring for at the age of seven.

This child was one of the first to be assigned a sponsor through the documents we were filling out. He is smiling because we just told him he would be cared for. In such difficult circumstances, I was grateful to bring good news and joy through sponsorship, meals, love, and the gospel.

A Baby in an Outhouse

Reader discretion advised

Because of the difficult economic situation in Jabana and other areas of Rwanda, as well as other nations where we are currently serving, we have come across many cases where children are suffering. That is what broke my heart on the first trip, and it is what continues to motivate me and so many others today.

One of the most memorable children we have cared for is Mary Noela Mugisha. In 2007, she was dropped down the hole of an outhouse shack in Jabana, Rwanda, when she was only two days old. This beautiful little girl was literally thrown away! I cannot even imagine what her mother must have been going through to make such a desperate decision.

A neighbor woman came by later and heard the baby's cries. She went for help, and the baby was rescued from the hole in the ground. One of the local Home Church members offered to receive the baby

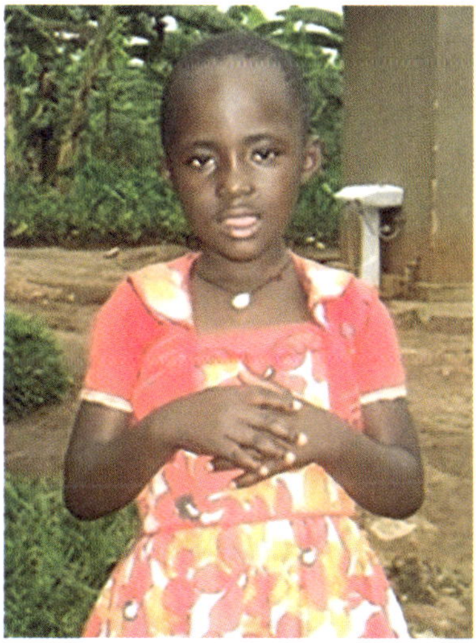

Left: Mary Noela a few years after being rescued
Right: today, age 14 (right, in green and yellow)

into her home to live with her family. A Canadian sponsor partnered with Home of Hope to help her care for the child financially.

This lovely girl is *alive* today because someone cared enough to rescue her, a family opened their doors to her, and another person's heart was touched to give money every month. Mary Noela is known for her compassion and her heart of gold. She adores going to school and is so thankful for every good thing in her life. She has a dream of becoming a doctor so she can help other abandoned babies.

Treat Them Like Royalty

I am so grateful to the hundreds of sponsors who have generously given their money, time, love, and faith to serve the children. Today, years after those first Jabana trips, it is so rewarding to see the children grown and full of hope.

Recently, for example, I was privileged to call the sponsor of a young man named Legis, one of our very first children, and tell him, "Thank you for sponsoring Legis for so many years. He has now finished his schooling and no longer needs monthly sponsorship. He is healthy, and he is a great young man. He is presently attending a vocational school where he is studying mechanics and learning to fix cars. He hopes to have his own car garage shop someday."

The sponsor was so overcome with emotion that he could not talk to me over the phone. He had to send me a text saying that he cried and cried, so grateful to have been able to play a part in helping Legis. He added that he wanted to sponsor another child. Of course I was crying by then as well.

My cousin, Mark Thomson, called me one day about the children that he was sponsoring. "Brian, I would like to do something more than monthly sponsorship. What could you do with $100 for each of my three sponsored children?"

Above: when we first met Legis, this was where he slept.
Below, left: Legis' sponsor card in 2016
Below, right: Legis in 2021

Rwanda

Legis Niyomwungeri

Your sponsorship provides food, water, clothing, medical care, Christian mentoring and attendance at church for this child.

Birthdate: 16-Mar-05 **Age:** 16 Male
City/Area: Jabana
Father Alive? No **Mother Alive?** Yes
Parent notes: Father died of malaria

Living With: Mother
Hobbies: volleyball
Health: good

Legis is a character! He is funny, charming and known for his caring heart. He loves his English class and learning new things. He is so interested in the world and all that is going on. He loves attending the Home Church Jabana, serving as an Usher.
His goal after finishing school, is to go to Mechanics school to learn how to fix cars, and dreams of owning his own mechanic shop.

I told him that there is never any pressure for any sponsor to buy anything extra for the children. He responded, "I remember you talking about a Bible verse that God is going to pick up orphans from the dirt and put them on thrones like princes. I want to treat my sponsored children like royalty because that is what they are!"

He was referring to 1 Samuel 2:8. "He raises the poor from the dust and lifts the needy from the ash heap; He seats them with princes and has them inherit a throne of honor" (NIV).

So, when my daughter Karissa went to Rwanda, her mission was to spoil his sponsored kids! She said that it was one of the highlights of her trip.

> **KARISSA:** *I was communicating back and forth between the sponsored children and Mark. Mark kept prodding me for more things he could do for them. He wanted to know what they wanted, not just what they needed. A bike or cool shoes or even a TV? I remember taking one of his sponsored children shopping. He needed help carrying in all the things Mark had bought him: a foam mattress, a big bag of food, sunglasses, a cool outfit, and more. His smile was radiant that day, and his posture changed. Someone in the world—someone across the world—loved him so much. His life changed that day, I'm sure of it.*

On Mission

Many people wanted to visit Rwanda with us and help in whatever way they could, so we organized trip after trip. I usually led three per year, and Elroy and other qualified Home Church leaders led teams as well.

We found many ways to connect volunteers with the needs in

Jabana. We took business people who could train local people in leadership skills. We introduced people to microloans, which I'll describe later. We began training caregivers to take care of the newly sponsored children in Jabana. These caregivers would make sure the kids received food and attended school. They would also shop for clothes, shoes, mattresses, and anything else that they needed.

Because so many people wanted to go on a trip to Rwanda, I created a two-hour missions class. It included simple things like getting your passport, saving money, what Rwanda was like, and what people could do to help.

Elroy Pankratz, the man who accompanied me on my first trip to Rwanda, joined me on several more trips. Eventually, he decided he wanted to live in Rwanda for a while! He and his wife, Nancy, stayed for many months. It was so fulfilling for him to see hundreds of people accepting Jesus. Elroy was a retired pastor, but he was also an experienced builder who later assisted in the construction of our church building in Jabana. Nancy was a nurse, and her skills and training were extremely helpful.

They both fell in love with Rwanda, and for many years, they were a powerful team. Elroy helped start our projects in Rwanda, Kenya, and Malawi, and he was also key in motivating me to start in the Democratic Republic of Congo (DR Congo). People from many countries of Africa loved Elroy and Nancy.

Elroy was seventy years young when he first went to Rwanda with me—his life changed drastically in his later years! He often told me his time in Rwanda was one of the greatest things he had ever done. Elroy's last trip with me was when he was eighty-two years old. Two years later, he went home to be with Jesus. All I can say is, "Well done, good and faithful servant of Jesus!"

My entire family has been a part of this work since the beginning, which makes me extremely happy. My wife, Connie, has helped greatly with administration. My sister, Florence, designed the computer program and sponsorship cards. All of my kids have sponsored children and gone on trips to visit them. I couldn't have done it without my family and all the countless hours they volunteered.

I never wanted to take a salary from Home of Hope, and I haven't to this day. I always desired that 100% of the funds raised would go directly to help the poor. But as the number of sponsored children in Rwanda approached 200, it was obvious that we would need to hire an administrator if we wanted to help more than that. It was becoming more and more complicated to collect sponsorship money, wire it over, and manage it well.

After many meetings and research into what other charities were doing regarding administration fees, we decided on a 10% administration fee from all the donations. This was a hard decision for me personally, but to help more children, it was the wisest way to move forward. That is when we hired our daughter, Karissa. She came on part-time after finishing Bible College, and later she became the full-time administrator, adding creativity and ideas to expand HOH to reach hundreds more children.

This entire ministry has been a wonderful partnership between people who know that both they and the children we serve are **Meant 4 More**. Sponsors and volunteers, young and old, Canadians and Rwandans, and later national teams in other nations as well—everyone works together to give dignity and hope to families in need.

5. LOVE IS CONTAGIOUS

Cyuru, Rwanda, and Beyond

KIGALI AND JABANA WERE ONLY THE BEGINNING. God stirred our local team to reach out to other areas of Rwanda, and people came from other villages to see what was happening in Jabana as well. The success of the child sponsorships and church planting efforts was inspiring.

In 2008, we took an evangelism team to the village of Cyuru (chu-ru), in the northern part of Rwanda, to help plant a Home Church there. (See the map on following page.) On our next trip, the pastor who was leading the work, Pastor Fidele Binyonyo, introduced us to fifty children in need. We began sponsoring those we could. That was the first time we extended beyond Jabana, and it became a model we followed many times over in multiple countries: helping children and the poor while preaching Jesus.

I love the way Jesus helped people. The Bible tells us that when He saw the multitude, He *taught* the people, then He *healed* them, and then He *fed* them. In other words, He met both their physical and spiritual needs. He ministered to their bodies and their souls.

Jesus said, "Go and make disciples of all nations" (Matthew 28:19 NIV). Over time, we planted churches in many other needy areas. We always tried to have an action plan to help the most disadvantaged children in the region surrounding those church-

es. This was part of the expanded version of God's will that I was discovering—preaching the Gospel in both word and deed and showing His love to people both spiritually and practically.

Home of Hope is not just a humanitarian organization, nor is it just a social outreach organization. It is both. We believe that bringing people to Jesus and teaching them the Bible are the best ways to help the poor, but we show them God's love in practical, tangible ways as well, meeting their spiritual and physical needs. In everything we do, we tell people about Jesus and introduce them to the Gospel. We plant churches with a strong focus on compassion and social outreach, and those churches are able to be incredibly effective in reaching their communities with the love of Jesus. Today we have twenty churches in Rwanda. We've sponsored hundreds of children, and we've fed many thousands more.

Sleeping among the Cows

Reader discretion advised

The following story from Cyuru shows how the love of God is both preached and demonstrated. It was also a life-changing moment for me.

When we go to a new area, we usually visit the local authority or village chief and say we want our church to be a blessing in their region. We ask if they know any desperate children who need help.

When we first went to Cyuru, the regional leader said, "Yes, there is a little girl named Jeannette whose mother died when she was two, and now she has nowhere to live."

I asked if I could meet her immediately. We found out later that she had been sleeping in the field with the cows to stay warm at night! One of the team members with me from Canada was a nurse, and as soon as the little girl arrived, our nurse spent time with her. She found bruises all over her body and believed that the girl was suffering mentally from harsh abuse and from being hit in the head many times.

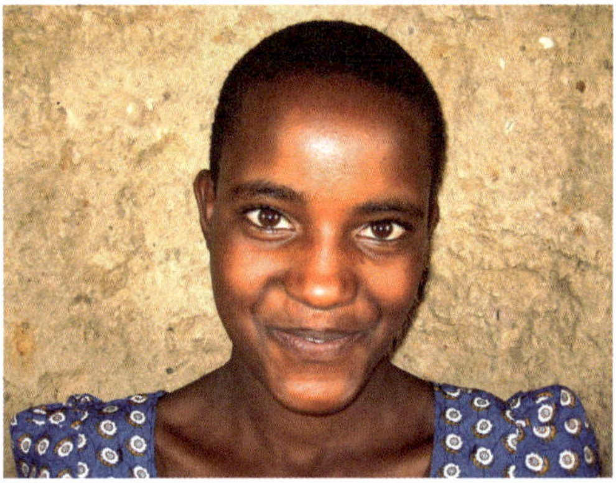

As we were meeting with her, we gave her as much healthy food as she could eat. She seemed ravenous. We also gave her new clothes. But what she loved the best was a stuffed animal that she hugged sweetly.

Pastor Fidele found a place where she could stay on the condition that we find someone who could sponsor her every month.

It was a great action plan between the local church and generous sponsors working together to save her life.

That evening at supper, the team was telling highlights of their day. When it was my turn, I recounted how the regional leader connected us to this young girl, and I began to weep. God had used us to rescue this girl today. I couldn't continue talking through the tears. God was again pouring more love into my heart, just as he had with those first four children in Kigali. It was a powerful moment for all of us. I spent hours kneeling on the floor that evening, praying and interceding with some of our team that God would use HOH to help more children like her.

Each time I traveled back to Cyuru after that, I asked to see Jeannette. God healed her! She got better mentally and physically, and she did well in school. A few years later, she wanted to show me something. She had saved some of the monthly sponsorship money to purchase her own goat, which then had twins. Over time she had grown a little herd. She had sold some of them and bought a pig.

A few years later, on another visit, she showed me that she had more goats, many pigs, and even a cow. She was so proud of that cow! Today, Jeannette is happily married with two children. She is a friend of mine, and we stay in contact online.

Pastors Fidele and Betty Binyonyo

I am so grateful for Pastor Fidele Binyonyo and his wife Betty, who taught Jeannette and other young people to earn and save their own money. Fidele and Betty have been with Home Church for over thirteen years and have done an outstanding job as the pastors of Cyuru. Fidele is now our national church and ministry overseer in Rwanda. They excel at teaching and training hundreds of people to come out of poverty and to become successful.

Single Mother Living at Police Station

Let me give you one more story of the power of compassion to change lives. The local leader in Cyuru asked us if we could help a lady with three young boys who was destitute and very sick. He was allowing them to sleep in a room at the village police station. Some people would bring a little food for her and her boys from time to time. The local leader told me that this lady had been a prostitute, and because of poor health, she had undergone several operations. She was so weak that she could no longer provide for herself and her children.

Of course we wanted to help! This woman had suffered so much, and we wanted to do whatever we could to give her hope and dignity. We sent a vehicle to pick her and her three sons up and bring them to the special meetings we were having with our team from Canada. Afterward, we fed them, gave them clothes, and found them a place where they could sleep. She took the business training we offered, and she was given some money to start a business.

This family is doing great today! The mother has a successful business, and all the boys are healthy and in school. When I go to this area, she is often sitting in the front row of church with a big smile, and she always comes over to greet and thank me. I am so glad that we were able to help them!

Don't Say No to God

God brought more and more people into the ministry. Many were sponsors, some became advisors on our HOH team, and others gave financially to the constantly growing work. I could only watch in amazement as people caught the vision that their lives, time, resources, and faith are **Meant 4 More**.

The story of my long-time friend Dan Peters is a good example of this. I remember speaking at Home Church in Olds, Alberta, which was a thirty-minute drive from my home in Red Deer. I gave my short presentation on Home of Hope, and then I moved on to my message from the Bible, preaching about Jesus, as I always do.

After the service, Dan came up to me and said, "Pastor Brian, I would like to donate to help you and your new project." He held out an envelope to me, but as I reached for it, he pulled it back and said, "I will give this money to you on one condition—that you will *never* ask me to go on a trip with you." He was serious. He went on to explain that he was busy with his business, he didn't ever want to be up on a stage, and he didn't want to go all the way to Rwanda just to spend time with children.

I replied, "Dan, I'll never pressure you into going on a ministry trip, but don't say no if God asks you to go." Dan smiled and handed me the envelope.

Not long after that, I was back in Olds, teaching our missions course and explaining what a Home of Hope trip involved. You can probably guess who was in attendance.

"Dan!" I said to him. "What are you doing here? I thought you weren't interested. This is a course about going on a ministry trip!"

He replied, "I know. I don't want to go, but I just thought I would attend your class and learn more about where my money is going."

That made sense. At the end of the class, during the question-and-answer session, Dan spoke up. "I don't want to go on one of these trips with you, but if I did, what would I do? I'm just a real estate agent."

I teared up immediately. "Dan, you could be so powerful!" I said once I regained my composure. "With your business mind, you could sit down with a small group of single mothers who are struggling to feed their children and teach them how to make money for their families."

Just a few months later, Dan decided to go on a trip with others from his church. It changed his life. Here is Dan's testimony of going to Rwanda for the first time.

> **DAN PETERS:** *Back in 2007, Pastor Brian had started projects in Rwanda, specifically building a duplex for orphans in a family unit with eight children and a caregiver. I felt that I wanted to contribute funds towards the project, and when I presented him with the funds, he said, "You should come with me to Rwanda."*
>
> *I quickly responded, "I need to go to Maui, not Rwanda." I thought that if I saw terrible poverty first-hand, I would end up being guilt-ridden for enjoying the prosperity and luxury of life in Canada.*
>
> *In a church service a few months later, my pastor, Ed Furst, announced that he was planning a ministry trip to Rwanda. He said he was looking for business people to go with him. He stated that Pastor Brian Thomson would be coming to Olds next week to teach an introductory course for people interested in going on the trip. I looked around at those in attendance and thought to myself, "Yes, some of these businessmen should go."*
>
> *That afternoon, I was reading a business-related book that said something like, "Instead of going on a vacation to Maui, as a business owner, you could consider going on*

> *a trip to an underdeveloped country to help people learn business skills."*
>
> *Almost immediately, my wife, Evelyn, walked into the room and randomly asked, "Don't you think you should go to that course?"*
>
> *That was it. "Okay, God! Fine! I'll go!" This seemed like the only logical and reasonable answer.*
>
> *I made plans for my first trip to Rwanda, and soon, I found myself in Jabana, Rwanda. I loved the warmth of the people and their eagerness to accept help. I got to experience the sheer joy of seeing people who had no hope now having hope for their lives. I got to see how a little can make such a huge difference.*
>
> *Well, it became addicting. I have gone over twenty-four times now—and counting.*
>
> *I didn't think I had much to offer, but I discovered the joy and fulfillment that come from helping others. It is a privilege to serve the poor and underprivileged. It has given me vision and determination to see my business succeed so I can continue to go on many trips to Africa and other places, doing what I now love to do.*

Dan came home beaming from his first trip to Rwanda. Every picture that he showed me was of him surrounded by children. He looked so happy being in Rwanda. They loved touching his white skin and hairy arms. I think those children changed his heart. After that, he wanted to go on another trip, and then another trip. To my surprise, this man who never wanted to be on stage fell in love with sharing the Gospel of Jesus in outdoor meetings, and he saw many people respond to the invitation to ask Jesus into their lives.

I invited Dan to become part of the HOH advisors team. He gave us practical advice as the projects started to grow, and he has

helped so many people through his generosity. Almost every time I see him, he says something like, "Brian, I want to go back. Here are the dates that work best for me, and this is what I would like to do in this country, and then I want to go over to that other country..."

It was exciting to see the change in Dan, the new fire and excitement, and, most of all, the purpose of God unfolding in his life. Dan found out that he was **Meant 4 More.** He has motivated many other people to follow his example and to live for Jesus by helping others and even going on teams that Dan has led.

Update on the Original Four

Before concluding this chapter and continuing with the story of Home of Hope in other nations, let me share with you a recent update that was sent to me by Emmanuel Tuyishimire, the boy I sponsored (and whose card I had to hide from visitors to my house!). He was twelve years old at the time but looked much younger. At the time of this writing, he is twenty-six years old, and he helps our teams by translating for them. He loves teaching children and youth in our Home Churches in Rwanda. He has finished his bachelor's degree in finance as well. I make sure I visit Emmanuel on every trip to Rwanda. I am so proud of him!

> **EMMANUEL:** *When I was young, I was very sad when I lost my father. I had no choice but to help care for my younger siblings because my mother was in the hospital. We had nothing to eat. I met Pastor Brian when he came to visit us at our mud hut. Because of God's love in using him to help us, we were all able to eat and go to school!*
>
> *Today, 14 years later, we are all doing great! My older sister, Marie Claire, is 29 and married. They are doing well with a business selling rabbits and chickens. My younger sister, Josiane, is 18 now and graduated high school in 2019. She wants to go to college for business. My younger brother, Eric, is 15 and*

has four years of school left. He wants to be a doctor. He is a very good artist as well!

The three of us live in a house on the Jabana Home Church property. I received help to attend university because of Home of Hope. Now I am working as a volunteer in the Home of Hope national office because they did great things for me, and maybe I can now help other kids who need a place to live or food to eat.

I want to always keep praying for Pastor Brian and Home of Hope because they changed my life and other kids' lives. I love you so much, Pastor Brian.

The original four, April 2021: Josiane, Marie Claire and her husband Bernard, Eric, and Emmanuel.

6. HOW TO SPEND A LAYOVER

Nairobi, Kenya

I HAVE A CONFESSION: I DON'T REALLY LIKE TRAVELING. This is hilarious because I travel for a living. Clearly, God has a sense of humor.

I have another confession: I'm a bit of a workaholic. One of the hardest things for me to do on any trip is sit for hours on a plane or waste half a day on a layover. This is also hilarious because, as anyone who has traveled internationally knows, there is a lot of waiting and wasted time involved in that process. So, I always try to find something productive to do.

In retrospect, my inability to just sit back and relax on a layover indirectly led to our first work outside of Rwanda, which was in Nairobi, Kenya. This would eventually grow into a huge part of Home of Hope's compassion ministries, but of course, nobody knew that at the time. Here's how it happened.

I mentioned earlier that we began organizing regular trips to Rwanda after that initial trip in 2006. For the first few years, that trip would take over forty hours from our city in Canada to the hotel in Rwanda. In large part, that was because of the layovers. We would often have a ten-hour layover in London, then a seven-hour layover in Nairobi, Kenya, before finally catching a connecting flight to Kigali, Rwanda.

On one trip in 2007, rather than sitting bored at the airport for seven hours, I decided to reach out to a friend I had made on a previous trip to Kenya many years before. He invited me to go with him during my layover for a quick meeting with some people who were not attending any church and were interested in learning more about Home Church.

I landed in Nairobi. It took over an hour to get through security to leave the airport. By now, I was getting nervous. I wondered if I would have enough time to do everything we had planned. But at least I was going to be doing something productive and not just be sitting in a busy airport! We got in a car and headed out for the meeting.

This was my first encounter with the terrible traffic jams in Nairobi. It was the worst traffic I had ever seen. It seemed like drivers would go wherever they could fit, whether there were lanes or not. There was lots of honking, bumpy roads, and potholes. It was intense. Our driver was a pro, though. We dodged the traffic jams by taking detours (and even driving through a few ditches!) until we finally made it to the rented hall for the meeting where about ten people were waiting for us. I introduced the vision that God gave me to start churches in Africa. I also shared our Home Church history, mission statement, and core values, answered lots of questions, and prayed with them.

They told me about the many slums in the city. I had never heard of anything like it. It was quite a culture shock for me. Over a million people lived in the largest slum, and conditions were inhumane, violent, and desperate. I'll explain more about how we began serving babies, children, women, and families in the slums in a later chapter. They shared the frustration of trying to start a church in such a challenging environment.

This team had amazing people with calling and passion, and their abilities were obvious. They were surrounded by great need and they knew God had called them to help those who lived there.

However, they were discouraged that they had not seen the fruit in their ministry and church that they knew they should. They asked me many questions, and I gave some suggestions to consider.

We finished the meeting and started the journey back to the airport. Again, my patience and prayer life were tested by the traffic chaos! We did make it back to the airport on time, in case you were wondering. The stress and nerve-wracking moments were worth it. I'd rather navigate life-threatening traffic and preach in a slum than sit bored in an airport any day!

I was excited about the new relationships I formed that day, and I looked forward to working with them as the foundation to start a new Home Church. I encouraged them to start meeting privately on Sundays as a core team and listen to our training materials together. I felt the Lord leading me. It was a divine connection.

Beginning in Nairobi

It was clear to all of us that God was connecting us for something great for the future. So, we planned that every time I traveled to Rwanda and had a layover in Nairobi, we would meet and keep the relationship going. That was the beginning of a two-year process of weekly, long-distance discipleship, along with regular meetings with the team in Nairobi.

This was happening at the same time as our work in Rwanda was growing in Jabana, Cyuru, and throughout the nation. In those early years, I didn't have any idea what the future held for Kenya. I just knew that this team had a heart to serve the people in need around them, and I wanted to help them with whatever training and encouragement I could give them.

As mentioned before, Dan Peters loved his first trip to Africa and wanted to go back. So, he agreed to have a layover in Nairobi to meet the group of people. He went with his pastor, Ed Furst. Here are their stories.

> **DAN PETERS:** *The first time I met this Kenyan team, I was so excited. I was in Kenya doing my best to encourage and build the team. I found out that one of the team had walked seven hours to get there because he had no money for a taxi or bus. I was astounded at how significant that was. He made an incredible sacrifice to be there.*
>
> *I have spent so much time with many of the people in this team. And now to see what the Church and Home of Hope has grown into is so amazing. Some of the team risk their lives in high-pressure situations to rescue babies, while other team members who are full of the love of God care for the abandoned children. It is wonderful to see people who choose to be selfless and do what is in the best interest of children and not themselves. I loved Kenya so much that now I go back and forth to Kenya and other countries on a regular basis, and I especially love the rescued children at the Dream Centre.*

Over the next two years, every team that went to Rwanda stopped over in Nairobi to do extra training. Many pastors from Canada have taken trips to provide training for this new project.

ED FURST: *Our church in Olds, Alberta, Canada was on board right from the start and raised finances to send me to Jabana, Rwanda. Pastor Brian asked us to stop over in Kenya on the way and speak with the team that was forming. We were so inspired to see these courageous individuals—a team that was willing to face the challenges and dangers of going where others did not want to go, even putting their own lives at risk for those in desperate situations.*

Ed and Kaleb

Walking through the slum, it was hard to see people who had no food, no sanitation, no sense of safety, and no way to change it. I thought how the small amount I spend on coffees each month in our budget would change their lives dramatically. I wanted to tell the church back home how we could get started in the work, partnering with the local leaders we were getting to know! We couldn't help everybody, but we could help a good number of people if we worked together. We are happy to see our sponsored children looking so strong, healthy, and happy. Our Kenyan and Rwandan kids became part of our expanding extended family.

It became a family affair as I traveled back again with my wife Melissa, then again with my mother Margaret, and most recently with my son Kaleb. How awesome it was for my nineteen-year-old Canadian son to meet his nineteen-year-old Rwandan brother.

Home Church Nairobi

We continued with our weekly online training, and we had many phone conversations about how we could help people in the slum. We decided that the best place to plant a church was next to the slum, not in it, because everybody wanted to get out of that place. It was not a good place to live, and they needed hope that they could have a better life.

In 2010, we officially started a Home Church in Nairobi, near the Korogocho slum. We also began sponsoring children and working with our leaders to serve people in the several slums in Nairobi, including rescuing unwanted babies who were left to die and starting the Dream Centre, which I'll talk about in another chapter.

Slum in Nairobi

Currently, there are fourteen Home Churches in Kenya, and we are starting more this year. One of our churches has about 450 people in attendance. Some of the original group of people we began discipling after that Nairobi layover are now pastors of Home Churches, often located next to the slums to help people. We are also sponsoring over 250 children in Kenya alone, as well as feeding hundreds more each week.

Since my first trip nearly fifteen years ago, much has changed in Nairobi. The Kenyan government has been implementing plans to modernize traffic management. They have been expanding highways, revamping the train system, and upgrading roads to improve transportation. I'm sure the terrible traffic menace will soon be a thing of the past!

There have also been improvements in and around the slums. There has been significant intervention by the Kenyan government to improve infrastructure and provide essential services for many households, including things like roads, drainage, lighting, water, sanitation, health, education, and even recreation facilities. This has been an ongoing work in the Kibera and Korogocho slums, as well as others. There is still much to do, but we are grateful to the government and other organizations who are continually working toward a better quality of life for the people of Nairobi, and we are happy to participate and serve alongside our team.

As the work in Kenya and Rwanda grew, little did I know that God was about to speak to me about doing something I could never have imagined, something that would challenge the faith and creativity of our growing team to its core.

7. THE ORIGINAL HOME OF HOPE

India

DURING THE FIRST YEARS OF OUR WORK IN RWANDA AND KENYA, my friend and mentor, Katherine Hoover, asked me on a couple of occasions to consider taking over her role as director of the Home of Hope orphanage in India. I turned her down because I was too busy with the rapidly growing work.

In 2010, Katherine asked me once again if I would take over leadership of the HOH in India. She could no longer travel as much as before, and she didn't have the energy to oversee fundraising and keep the orphanage going. She talked with Pastor Mel Mullen as well, and she said that she would sign over all ownership of the property on the condition that I would be the director. This time, I couldn't say no! Bob and Katherine were right, of course. As usual, it seems everyone around me knew what I was going to do before I did! The orphanage and property were transferred to Home Church, and I became the overseer.

Bob and Katherine had partnered with a man named Moses when they had started the orphanage in India. Moses had trained his grandson, Andrew Paul, to become the director. So both Andrew and I stepped into new roles together. It was such a divine transfer from Grandpa Moses to his grandson and from my beloved mentors to me.

The Legacy Continues

Andrew and I became instant friends. It was clear that God's grace was on us to work together. I count it a privilege to work with friends, not just members of an organization.

I love how Jesus called His disciples to follow him, but then He called them His friends. "I no longer call you servants, because a servant does not know his master's business. Instead, I have called you friends, for everything that I learned from my Father I have made known to you" (John 15:15 NIV).

> **ANDREW:** *After Bible College, I was not confident. As a twenty-year-old, I had to work with people who were older and more experienced than me as the new Home of Hope leader. Some were extremely hard to lead. But Pastor Brian told me, "When God raises you up, you must move with confidence and His authority into what He wants you to do." Pastor Brian offered to meet with me online every*

Thursday, and he has traveled many times to India to be with us. He changed my life and influenced me to be the best leader I can be.

Today, I feel I have grown so much. I have become a good leader, and Home of Hope India is healthy and growing. I am also the pastor of a strong village church and have a vision to start more Home Churches in India. Because of Brian's mentoring, I can speak in front of hundreds and even thousands of people without fear. Eleven years ago, I could only speak in the shower, but never in front of people. I had a dream of someday being bold and speaking in front of large crowds. I am a strong leader and have a big vision for what I feel God has called me to do.

I am so proud of Andrew and how he has grown in the Lord. He has faced many challenges, including monsoon storms, government interference that threatened to shut down the orphanage, and many intense death threats.

I enjoy working with teachable people like Andrew, and I try my best to see the unique gifting and calling for their lives. I am known for pushing and prodding people into their calling, and I always try to give words of encouragement and coaching to move step by step into the greater things God has for their lives.

Paul wrote in 1 Corinthians 14:3, "But one who prophesies strengthens others, encourages them, and comforts them"

(NIV). The word "encourage" means to urge forward or to persuade. One definition I found says "to prod." Andrew can testify to how much I care for him, and he can testify that he has needed a prod and a push in the right direction at times! He has needed coaching and mentoring. Other times, facing the trial of serious death threats, he has needed prayers and strength.

I don't believe any of us can fulfill all that we are called to be without the input of others. We all have blind spots and need others who love us and point things out to us. Can we remain teachable? Can we respond to the input of others? Coaching, mentoring, and even pruning often bring breakthrough. In a later chapter, I will share some practical suggestions to move to the next level in fulfilling God's purpose for our lives.

Andrew is now happily married to his wife, Ruth. They have two lovely daughters. They all live at the HOH India property. Andrew and Ruth are true heroes. Their dedication and selflessness are changing lives forever.

Here are two stories of rescuing orphans and abandoned children in India, as shared by Andrew. (*Reader discretion advised.*)

> **ANDREW SHARES VISHWA'S STORY:** *I love being the Home of Hope leader in India. My motivation when I started was that I wanted to help change the lives of the young boys. To my surprise, the boys have changed me. As we do God's will, we think we will help others, but we find that they have helped us even more.*
>
> *One day, I was traveling into the big city using the metro train. At the big train station, I saw a poor young boy, about seven years old. He was digging in the garbage to find something to eat. He looked so lost and hungry. I thought that he might live nearby, but when I*

returned to the metro to go home, I saw him again. I decided to go over to talk to him.

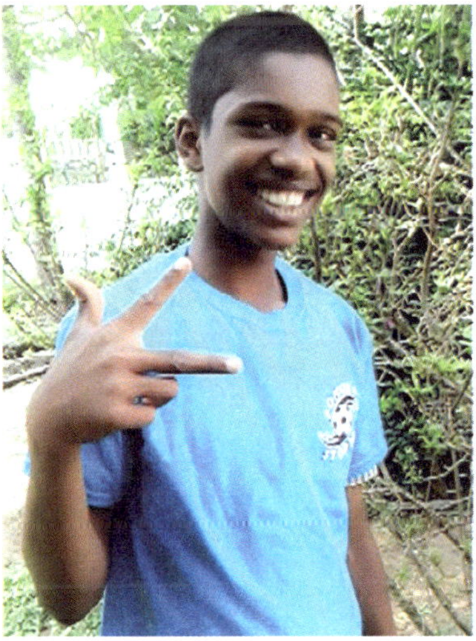

He told me his name was Vishwa. He explained to me that his father had died and that his mother told him, "You look ugly, and I don't want you anymore!" His mother told him that she wanted to get married again and that having an "ugly child" would hinder her from getting a husband. She then chased him out of their home!

Vishwa had been eating garbage for three weeks and had been sleeping under the train bridge. He led me back to his house, and I confirmed that his mother indeed did not want him, and even the grandmother said she did not like him. His mother signed a custody paper to give us permission to move him into the Boys Home of Hope. Throughout this process, I never thought he was ugly in any way. It seemed so foolish that a mother would believe her own child was ugly.

Vishwa has been living at the Home of Hope for nine years now. He is sixteen and so handsome. His goal is to go to college and get a degree as an accountant and work in a bank. His life is forever changed, and God has healed him from the terrible rejection of his family. I am so thankful to be part of HOH and to see desperate children's lives changed.

ANDREW SHARES JACOB'S STORY: *I loved Jacob so much from the first day I met him. Jacob came to Home of Hope when he was one and a half years old. His mother had been sexually assaulted at age twenty, and she became pregnant. Her parents found out about this, and they rejected her! Her parents' rejection was too much for this young, pregnant girl, and it affected her emotionally.*

She had a mental breakdown and ended up roaming around the streets begging and not even knowing her own name. It was so sad. One of the local store owners found Jacob going through the garbage close to their store, and they brought him to us. Now he is such a great young man, age seventeen. This year he will finish high school. Then he wants to go to college, and he plans to become a banker.

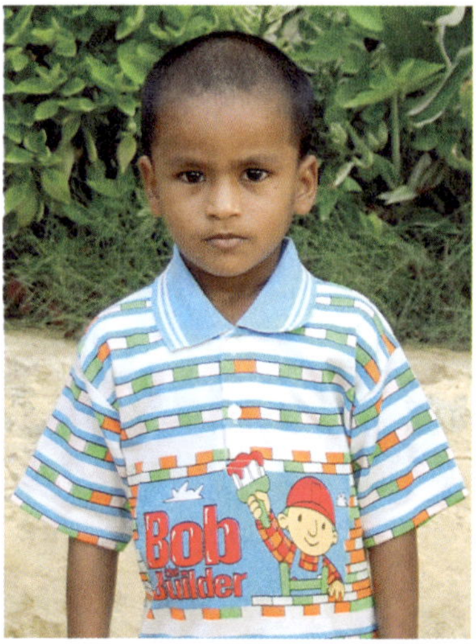

Left: Jacob soon after being rescued. Right: Jacob today, age 17.

One of the wonderful things Andrew has done is teach the boys at HOH to get up early and do chores around the property. They grow peanuts and rice, and they raise goats and cows. They also have group devotions and make sure their homework is done every day. Andrew's goal is to teach all the boys to work hard in their teen years and save for their own college fees. Sponsors have helped monthly with their food and clothes, but he believes that they must learn to work for themselves.

Andrew purchased a brick-making machine and taught Jacob and two other boys how to make and sell bricks to build up their business skills. Jacob told Andrew, "Home of Hope is my family. I am with Home of Hope forever." He is so thankful for his Canadian sponsors, who have supported him for twelve years. Here is their story, in their own words.

> **RON AND GLORIA:** *Sponsoring Jacob has certainly broadened our worldview! We love to hear stories about him when members from our church visit HOH India. Jacob was five when we started sponsoring him, and now he is a young man.*
>
> *It is always exciting for us to pick out gifts to send to him with the teams that go over. We start shopping for him weeks ahead. It feels like Christmas to us, and we want to show him our love by doing that. With those packages, we send letters, and what a delight it is to receive updates, video greetings, or a personal note from him in response. It warms our hearts. We pray for him regularly, and we feel so blessed to have been used in changing his life.*

Beach Days and Ice Cream

I've found that some people are intimidated by the idea of serving orphans, desperate children, and needy families. They seem to think that it requires incredible sacrifice or self-discipline or some impossible level of holiness. But it's not hard at all! When you invest time and attention in people who are in those difficult circumstances, you realize how joyful and fulfilling it is to be the hands, feet, and face of God's love.

The Bible says that we are to "visit the fatherless" (James 1:27 KJV). One time I studied what the word "visit" means in the original Greek. Do you know what it means? It literally means to visit! Amazing. It's just not that complicated.

I remember my first trip to India as the new overseer of the Boys Home of Hope. As we were driving from Chennai to the village of Kuzhipanthandalam (good luck sounding that out correctly), we passed by the beaches of the Sea of Bengal.

I asked, "How often do the boys get to go to these beautiful beaches?" I was surprised to hear that the boys had *never* been to the beach! What? It was only ten minutes away from the HOH property, and they had never been there?

It was only about six cents per person to ride on the public bus transportation from Kuzhipanthandalam (okay, I'll help you this time: Koo-lee-pan-tan-dal-am) to the closest beach. When I heard this, I *had* to take them to the beach! I promised the boys it would be so much fun.

The day came, and we took the bus to the beach. When we arrived, some of the boys were terrified. The huge expanse of water and the waves rolling back and forth scared them. A few of the boys walked slowly to the ocean and gingerly put their feet in the water. Mere seconds later, of course, they were running, jumping, and playing with huge grins plastered on their faces. I had brought along some balls and water toys, which added to the fun.

I noticed one four-year-old boy hanging far back from the ocean's edge, still stunned by the situation. I tried to coax him to get closer to the water. He stepped back and started to cry. So, I picked him up and, with an interpreter, explained to him, "There is no reason to be scared. Look at the boys playing. Doesn't it look like fun?" I took a few baby steps toward the water, but he did *not* want me to go any further. Then I took a few more. After about ten minutes of talking and slowly advancing, we reached the water.

I lowered him gently and let his toes touch the water. He still would not let me put him down. But just a few minutes after that, he was running and playing with the other boys! He ran and played so hard that his swimming shorts kept falling. He didn't care. He just kept running and playing with the other boys until we had to go. I couldn't help but smile—it brought so much joy to watch the boys experience a beach for the first time.

Of course, we had to get ice cream after the beach. That was a rare treat! I will never forget that great day. I was so happy to spend time with the orphans and give them an experience they, too, will never forget. Every trip since then, they always ask me to take them to the beach and for ice cream.

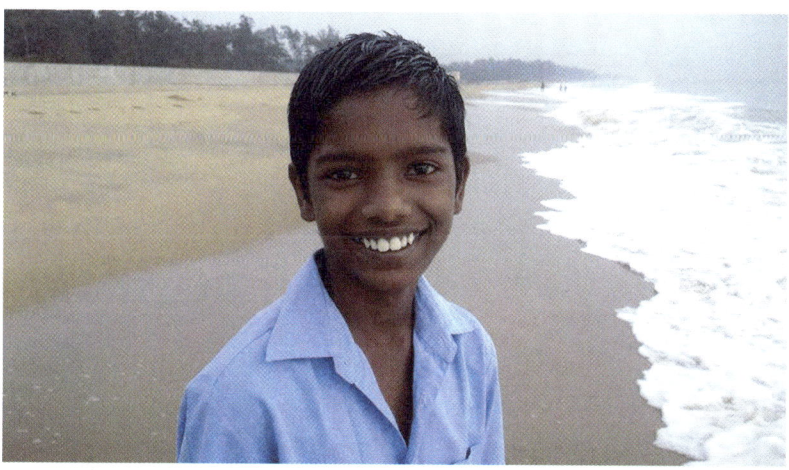

It is so much fun to obey the Bible—to visit the orphans and find fun things to do with them. Anyone can do this. Some people are so fearful of going on trips like this. They tell me that they don't want to preach or stand on the stage and tell their story, but then I tell them that the Bible says to visit the fatherless. Anyone can *visit*. It has been especially precious to have fathers with me who spend time visiting, loving, and teaching the children about Jesus. Here is one father's story.

> **SHAWN:** *On my first trip to India, everything I saw impacted me deeply. It amazed me that the people were so kind, and they loved us like we were family.*
>
> *The most impactful moment on my trip was meeting my sponsor boy, Phongau (Pong-go), who we had been sponsoring for a few years. His sponsor card is on our refrigerator, and we pray for him every day as a family. When I had the opportunity to meet him in India, I was flooded with emotions. I remember driving through the front gate of the orphanage, and the boys came running up to the van. I can clearly remember the first time Phongau and I locked eyes. We couldn't speak the same language, but we immediately knew who each other was and that this was a special and powerful moment.*
>
> *It was such an honor for my family and me to be part of seeing his life restored through Jesus and the church. It was also so good to build friendships with*

Phongau and the boys. As a father to two teenage boys myself, I especially loved the opportunity to bless the boys and be a "father" to them while I was there. I'd chat with them one-on-one and sit around in a circle, talking about their lives and the challenges that they were going through. I would tell them that Jesus loves them and that God has a great purpose for their lives and wants them to succeed.

The two trips to India I experienced were both very impactful for me, and I am so grateful to have met Phongau. We love him so much!

Staff Training

Part of working with children is training the staff and volunteers who are involved with their day-to-day caregiving. That means teaching them how to serve the children and create a safe environment where they can thrive. The culture of the Bible is higher than any culture of any country. I always want to teach the Bible as our standard of life.

All cultures in every nation need to change and adjust to the Bible. I am careful never to teach Canadian culture, but Bible culture.

On one of my first trips to India, I was sitting in a circle teaching some six- and seven-year-old boys with one of the staff interpreters helping. I told them that God has created all of us with a purpose and that we are on this planet for a reason. Jesus at age twelve knew what He was called to do. I asked the boys, "What do you think you will want to do as a vocation after you finish school? What do you think God's purpose is for you?"

One by one, they spoke up. Then one boy said, "I want to be a doctor!"

I couldn't believe what happened next. The interpreter instantly became angry and yelled, "You are an orphan! You will always be an orphan!" He slapped the boy's head and added, "You will never be a doctor. Stop thinking like that. You are an orphan!"

I was stunned. I had never seen anyone on our teams treat a child like that, much less a staff member, and I wasn't going to stand for it. The first thing I did was comfort the boy, then I asked the group to stay there while I took the interpreter aside. I was very upset with him! I asked him, "What are you doing? Why did you do that?"

He replied, "In our culture, we believe once an orphan, always an orphan. That is God's assignment for them."

I told him very firmly, "We are going to have a staff meeting to discuss this more. But you will never slap another child like that, or you will resign and leave the property immediately. Jesus loves children. He would never slap a child!"

I was still furious, but the boys were waiting. I asked for a different interpreter, and I went back to the circle. I continued telling them more scriptures about God's purpose. I told the boy who had spoken up, "If you want to be a doctor, you can be a doctor. The Bible is full of stories of people like you who had dreams. In fact, I know many doctors in Canada, and I believe some would come to

India to talk to you and probably even help you reach your dream."

The staff member who had slapped the child resigned soon after that. Over the next few days, we trained the staff for many hours on how the Bible instructs us to raise children. That week, the team with me helped me write a handbook for the staff. In all the HOH locations, we take our responsibility very seriously to not only meet their physical needs, but to treat them as Jesus would and to create a safe environment where they can dream, learn, and grow into the calling God has for them.

Found in a Field

Reader discretion advised

One of the first things I did when I assumed leadership of the Boys HOH was to get each boy sponsored like we were doing in Rwanda and Kenya. There were about sixty boys in the home. My pastors, Mel and Heather Mullen, wanted to sponsor a child, and they asked if any of the orphans happened to be named Robert, since that was Bob Hoover's name.

"Yes," I said, "There is a little boy named Robert." Robert had been found abandoned in a field at the age of three. His parents were nowhere to be found. He was brought to the HOH orphanage. We found out later that Robert's mother had died, and his father was paralyzed.

Pastors Mel and Heather have had the joy of sponsoring Robert (pictured on the next page) for many years, and they also helped him through medical school. Robert is now a successful nurse at a nearby clinic and serves on the team at the HOH property.

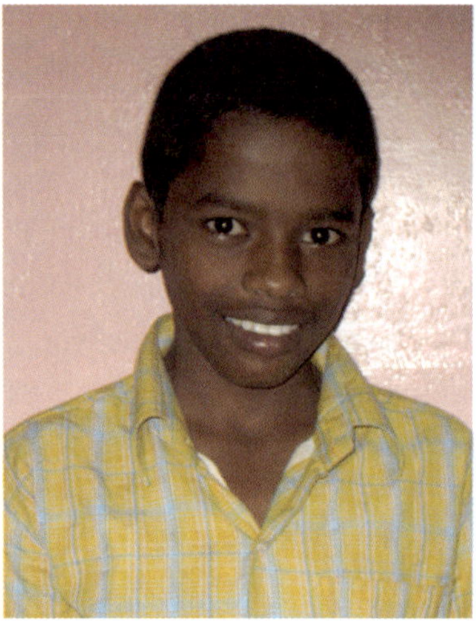

Robert as a child, a few years after beginning his sponsorship, and today, a successful nurse on staff at HOH.

Orphan Girls

Our orphanage is not allowed to have girls on site, so we have raised monthly sponsorship for orphaned or abandoned girls who stay in the homes of some of our church members in the village. The first orphan girl we helped had a drunk father who left the family when she was young, and he was never seen again. Years later, her mother died of cancer.

One of the families of our local church offered to let her sleep in their house. A dear friend of mine for over forty years called me the same week and said, "Brian, I was praying about you and Home of Hope today, and I thought I would ask you what your present need is."

I told him, "Today, I heard that a sweet teenage girl in India just lost her mother and has no hope.

He quickly said, "My wife and I would like to sponsor her!"

God is so good! The girl was so thankful that a sponsor helped with her basic needs every month. Today she is a successful young woman. She has finished her nursing degree and is married, and she visits HOH often. She is just one example of many young girls being cared for through HOH India and our church in the nearby village.

Looking Forward

At the time of writing this book, our HOH India orphanage is in the process of being converted into a boarding school. The government of India is not allowing orphanages to continue, but it will allow us to have a boarding school for orphans. We are constructing school buildings and enlarging the vision to become a day school for hundreds of students from the area. Along with the usual subjects, we will also teach English and biblical principles.

The bricks for the new buildings are being made by the older boys who have graduated and are earning money for their college education. Phongau, for example, is raising money to go to a fashion college, while Jacob is going to college so he can work in a bank.

As with all our locations, HOH India owes so much to the generosity of sponsors, volunteers, and the local staff. One incredible example of this generosity is Judy Dorken, Bob and Kay Hoover's daughter, who first visited India with her parents in 1985. Since then, she has been to India thirty-three times! When she saw what her parents were building, including the HOH property and the vision to help orphaned boys, a fire ignited in her heart. She was not afraid to travel and she has always loved adventure. Over the years, she helped raise money for the orphanage and the many projects.

There is information at the end of this book about how to get involved if you would like to do so, or you can visit www.homeofhope.ca for up-to-date information and current needs. From Rwanda to Kenya to India and beyond, there are so many ways to show God's love to children and families!

8. RESCUING BABIES

Nairobi, Kenya

Due to the topic of this chapter, reader discretion is advised.

When I visited the slums of Nairobi, Kenya for the first time during that layover in 2007, I could never have foreseen what would happen a few short years later. I mentioned earlier that we helped start a Home Church location in 2010 near the Korogocho slum. We also began sponsoring children and finding other ways to feed and care for kids and families in the Nairobi area, especially in the slums.

In December 2010, something happened that dramatically impacted the direction of the work in Nairobi. We heard about a news report that some of our team had seen on TV. The report said that babies were being thrown away in the biggest dump in the city, a landfill of over thirty acres. The report estimated that twenty babies a month were being thrown away like garbage!

We were deeply moved by the need, and we resolved to do what we could to help. We began discussing what we could do. It was heart-wrenching, tragic, and unbelievable. We had to find ways to save these babies. They were **Meant 4 More.**

At the start of every year, our church in Red Deer, Alberta, has a day of prayer, and our international leaders often join by video conferencing or by phone. January 7, 2011, was one of those days. We started praying for our international churches as usual. When we came to the prayer requests for Kenya, we reported to the group of about seventy-five people, "We have been discussing

with the team that we need to do something about the babies that are being abandoned in the city dump."

The people in the room were shocked by this prayer request. Babies were being thrown away in a dump? As we began to pray, there was such a strong presence of the Holy Spirit. Later, I met with the Kenya team and said, "Something happened at the prayer meeting. I felt it. Mark this day on the calendar because something big is coming. It is like the heavens just opened for Home of Hope Kenya."

As soon as I hung up the phone, a friend named Dawn came up to me and said, "Pastor Brian, it is so hard to believe that babies are thrown away. My husband Virgil and I want to be involved and help get this rescue ministry going. We want to help sponsor the workers who will be rescuing and caring for the babies."

I teared up and replied, "Thank you so much. I'm not sure what we will do, but I sure feel that the Lord wants us to start immediately." Her comment and generosity helped get the rescue project going, and they are still great supporters to this day. Virgil and Dawn Hrywkiw have both traveled to Kenya to see the project firsthand.

The Rescue Begins

One of our first action plans was to hire four local church members to walk through the dump early every morning, looking for babies who had been thrown away overnight. Even as I write these words, it is hard to imagine the desperation that would drive mothers or family members to abandon children. Later, we implemented strategies to reach out to those mothers and to provide alternatives, rather than leaving their babies to die; but at the beginning, we just wanted to rescue those we could.

Tragically, at first, the searchers found it impossible to rescue abandoned babies in time. The size of the dump, the harsh environment, and the wild animals were simply too much. However, while searching, they found very young children living in the dump. These children would eat the scraps of food they found from the truckloads of garbage that were dumped throughout the day. They used cardboard or torn tarps for their "beds."

One of the first children we rescued was a young boy who was about seven years old. He had been tied to a tree near the edge of the city dump. We found out that his parents had died. Unbelievably, his uncle and aunt didn't want him anymore, so they took him to the dump and tied him to a tree, leaving him to die. He was weak with malnutrition. We rescued him and started to care for and help him immediately!

We were still working on getting official papers from the government to keep the children we rescued, so the government took this child to an orphanage six hours away. We lost contact with him, but I still think of him often. His story impacted my next steps greatly. We picked up our pace and started to raise extra money to get the approval needed. Very soon, we had the legal permits necessary to house the children we rescued.

The Dream Centre

Within weeks of beginning our rescue ministry in the dump, in February of 2011, we received a donation to start renting a four-bedroom house that we furnished with beds, furniture, and kitchen utensils. We started by hiring one caregiver who could look after the first few children rescued from the dump. Pastor Jachin Mullen, the lead pastor of Home Church in Red Deer, went to see the rescue mission and cut the ribbon of this first rescue house. As we started rescuing more children, we rented a second house near the first one. One was for babies, and the other was for young children.

Around that time, Matthew Barnett, co-founder of the Los Angeles Dream Center, spoke at our Home Church. I had an opportunity to explain our rescue mission to him. I asked if we could use the name Dream Centre. He was delighted and said we could.

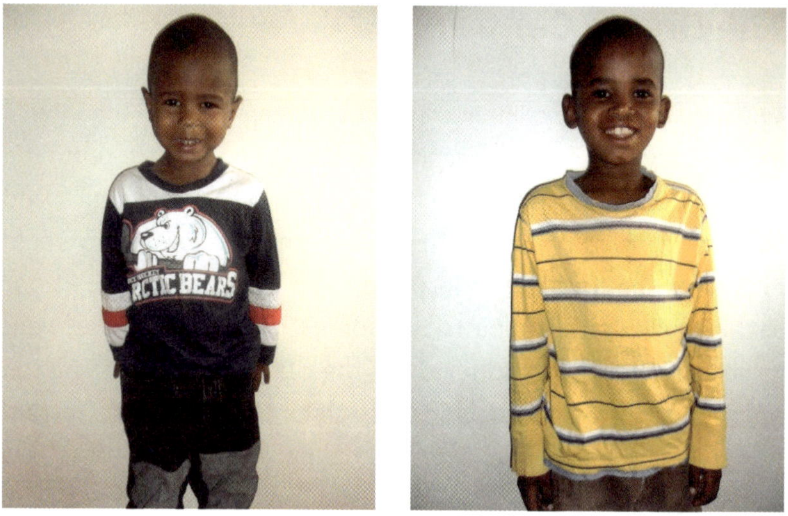

James (left) and Peter (right), a few years after being rescued.

Peter and James are two of the first children we rescued. In 2011, at the beginning of our ministry in the dump, the guards we had hired found them starving and cold in the dump. We discovered that their father died of HIV/AIDS and their mother abandoned them in the city dump, leaving them and their sick grandmother to fend for themselves. The three of them would look for plastic bags in the garbage to sell to buy food. Sadly, their grandmother also had HIV/AIDS and was hopeless, and she was considering whether to abandon James and his brother Peter. We asked if we could help, and Home of Hope began sponsoring the two boys.

Our goal was never to have lots of children living in an orphanage. The Bible says that "God sets the solitary in families..." (Psalm 68:6 KJV), and we always want to create environments that are as close to a home and family as possible. So, along with the Dream Centre, we implemented "family units," as we call them, where four to six children are placed into homes and become a family together with a caregiver couple.

Peter and James stayed at the Dream Centre at first, then became part of a loving family unit in 2013. According to their family, Peter is known today for being a responsible and kind young boy. He always tries his best, and he is at the top of his class. He is a young leader in the church and helps on Sundays by reading scriptures in front of the entire church. James loves playing soccer and wants to be a policeman and detective when he grows up. He has a very good appetite and eats everything! He also rarely catches a cold as his immune system is very good. He does very well in his studies and his teachers love him a lot. At home, he helps with house chores.

James and Peter are front and center, together with their adopted family unit.

Another young boy who was rescued in those early days is Jadon. Our Nairobi team heard about a baby boy, only nine months old, who had been locked inside a shanty in the slum for many days without food and water. He was so hungry that he had chewed and sucked on his fingers until all the skin came off. When he was rescued, all his fingers were bleeding, and he had to stay in the hospital for many days. It was terrible and heartbreaking.

He was then taken to the Dream Centre, where he was cared for and loved. A wonderful sponsor had the privilege of giving him his name and his new start to life. I love the name Jadon! It means "God has heard." His middle name, Amaziah, means "Strength of God," and his last name, Kibali, means "Favor."

On my next trip to the Kenya Dream Centre, Jadon was the first baby I looked for. It was such a joy to hug him, hold him, and pray for him. Now, every time I go back, I seek him out and spend extra time with him. The picture on the left was when he came home to the Dream Centre after being in the hospital. The picture on the right is five years later, when he was happy and healthy. Just like all the children we work with, Jadon is **Meant 4 More**.

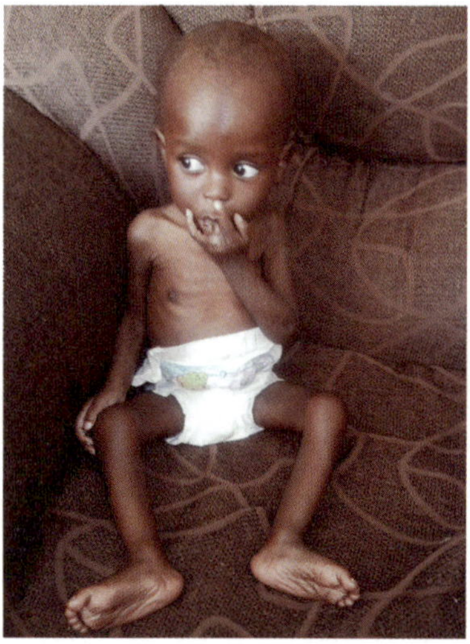

Another child we rescued is Benjamin. When he was four years old, he ran away from his abusive home and started picking through the dump for food. When he got tired, he slept in the rubbish. Finally, someone brought him to the Dream Centre. He smelled like garbage for a full week. Below is the location where the team found Benjamin. He was living there, alone, at only four years of age.

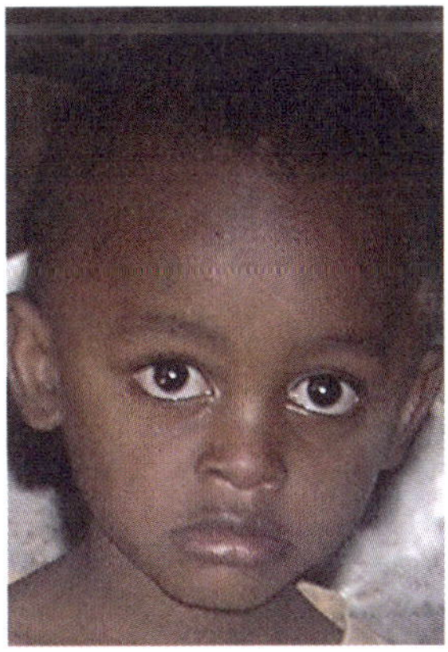

Rescuing Babies

As I mentioned earlier, we realized quickly that it would be nearly impossible to rescue babies thrown away in the dump due to the size and harsh conditions. The guards we had hired simply could not arrive in time. We needed something to prevent the babies from being thrown away in the first place.

We prayed and discussed the problem, and God gave us a creative solution. We made three ten-foot billboards telling people not to throw away their babies and offering to help them. We believed that if the mothers were offered an alternative, if we could give them hope, they would give their babies life.

We placed the signs high in the air at the entrances to the dump so they would be visible to many people. The phone started ringing. Those signs have prompted several calls every day for many years.

George and Janet Akelo are the rescue coordinators for abandoned babies in Nairobi, Kenya. The phone numbers on those three signs go to his cell phone.

> **GEORGE:** *The first time I met Pastor Brian, he prayed over me. It was over two years before we even had the idea of starting to rescue babies. As he prayed, he declared these words, "God is putting a burden on your shoulders to rescue babies and children. God is raising you up." Then he gave me this Bible verse: Isaiah 60:1-8, which talks about how God's presence would shine from my life to help people who are dwelling in deep darkness. I have read this Scripture almost every day since, and it continues to remind me that God has put this in my heart. This portion of Scripture motivates me to be a bright light to people in deep darkness.*

Samuel's Story

George was the one who responded when the first baby was rescued because of the billboards. In September 2011, shortly after the first of the three signposts was erected, he received a phone call. A baby had been left in a plastic bag by the bridge in the slum. Here is George's description of that day.

> **GEORGE:** *I ran as fast as I could. I didn't know if I was going to find the baby dead or alive. I was afraid that I was going to find another dead baby. And if it was alive, what was I going to do then? I arrived at the bridge and saw the baby in a plastic bag. He was still alive! The baby looked like he was only two hours old. He was shivering and cold because it was evening, and it was also drizzling. His umbilical cord was still attached. I picked him up, then I got a motorbike taxi and rushed to*

the hospital, shouting "Emergency" the whole way. When we arrived, the baby was rushed to an incubator, where he stayed for two or three days. When he was declared strong enough to move, we brought him back to the Dream Centre. The police gave us custody of him.

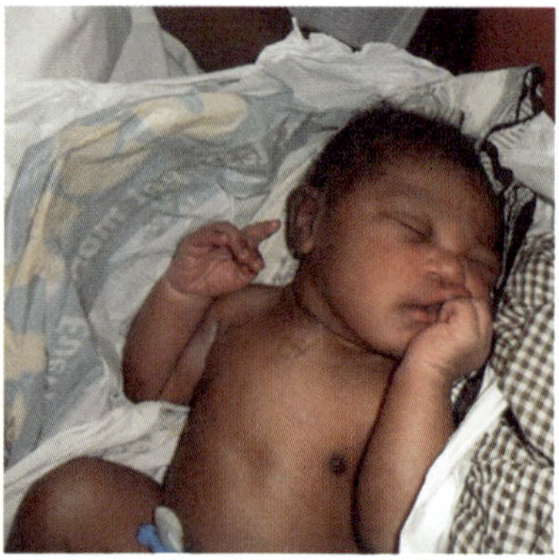

There were about seven children in the Dream Centre house at that time. The baby recovered quickly and began to do so well living there. He was given the name Samuel.

Now, when I run to rescue other children, I have this baby on my mind. God used me to save this child's life. I will never forget it! It gives me a passion to do what I do. Whenever I go to the Dream Centre, I look for Samuel to give him special attention, and I often take him out for ice cream.

The location where baby Samuel was found.

There is a passage in Ezekiel that reminds me of Samuel's story.

> On the day you were born, no one cared about you. Your umbilical cord was not cut, and you were never washed, rubbed with salt, and wrapped in cloth. No one had the slightest interest in you; no one pitied you or cared for you. On the day you were born, you were unwanted, dumped in a field and left to die.
>
> But I came by and saw you there, helplessly kicking about in your own blood. As you lay there, I said, "Live!" And I helped you to thrive like a plant in the field. You grew up and became a beautiful jewel.
>
> (Ezekiel 16:4-7 NLT)

At the writing of this book, Samuel is nine. I know God has great things in store for him!

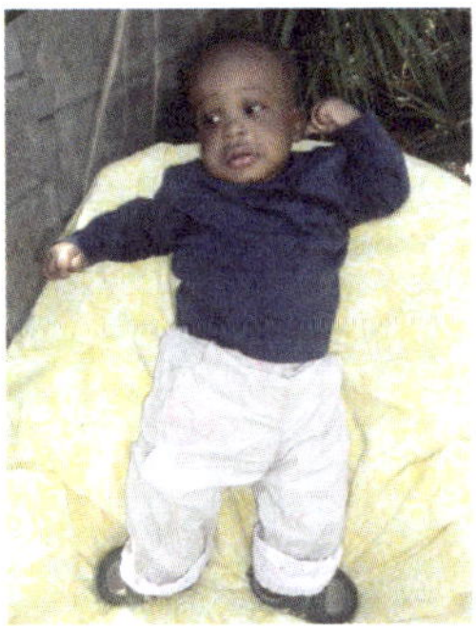

2012

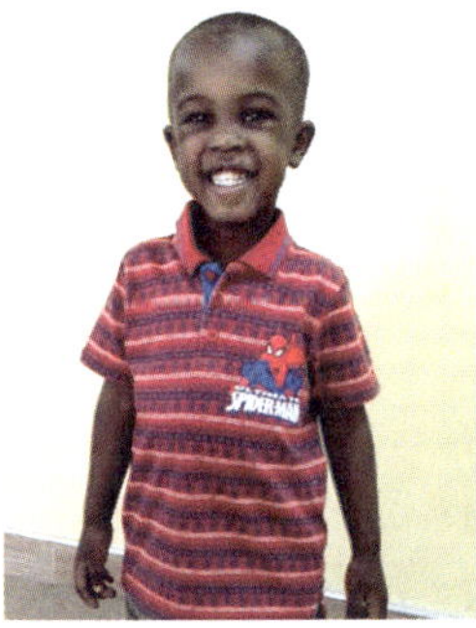

2015

2020

Samuel was not only the first baby we rescued in Nairobi, he was the first to be named by a sponsor. One of the things we hadn't thought of when we began rescuing babies was who would name them. When babies are abandoned, there is often no way of knowing anything about them. In these cases, we work together with the sponsors and the local Nairobi team to give them a name with a positive meaning that respects their heritage. Often the sponsor chooses the first name or names, and they select a Kenyan Swahili last name from a list suggested by the HOH staff in Nairobi.

At the beginning, we had no idea how significant this would be for the sponsors. They are thrilled to have such a special privilege because, for both the sponsors and the team in Nairobi, the babies are not anonymous, forgotten statistics but beloved human beings. Their names are such a crucial part of restoring the dignity and identity that they deserve.

Here is the story of Samuel's sponsors.

> **KATHARINE:** *My husband and I experienced an ectopic pregnancy, and it was very difficult to go through. I knew I wanted to get involved with one of the rescued babies if we couldn't have a baby of our own.*
>
> *One Sunday, we prayed together about sponsoring a baby, and that Friday, we were contacted from the Home of Hope office about a baby that had been thrown away with his umbilical cord still attached. They said we could name the baby!*
>
> *We felt that his name was especially important because he had been abandoned. I didn't want someone to tell him how he was born and for that to cause him not to have a feeling of importance. He is special, he is wanted, and he has a purpose and a destiny. I wanted to give that to him in his name.*
>
> *We chose the name Samuel Daudi Imani. "Samuel" means "God has heard" (because God heard our prayers), Daudi means "beloved," and Imani means "faith." Being able to help give life to a child who was left to be lifeless is an amazing thing to be a part of.*
>
> *Then, nine months later, I became pregnant again, and we had a healthy little boy! It was a miracle.*

We have heard several similar stories of women in Canada who could not have children, but after they started sponsoring a rescued baby, they became pregnant. God is a God of miracles, no matter what country or continent you live in!

Mothers' Hearts

As the Dream Centre began caring for more children, people in Canada asked to accompany us on our trips. They would say, "I want to go over to hug those babies and pray for them! Is there a rocking chair?" Yes, of course there were rocking chairs! And I was always excited to take people with me on teams to show love to the babies.

Connie has traveled with me a couple of times to see all that is happening. She is a terrific mother of four children and thirteen grandchildren, and she is always great with babies. She doesn't like traveling long distances either, but she wanted to hug the babies and help train the workers of this growing ministry.

Connie says, "Seeing the location where babies were thrown away, then going to the Dream Centre and hugging them was amazing. It was so hard to imagine that these struggling women living in the slum could come to such an extreme decision to throw away their babies!"

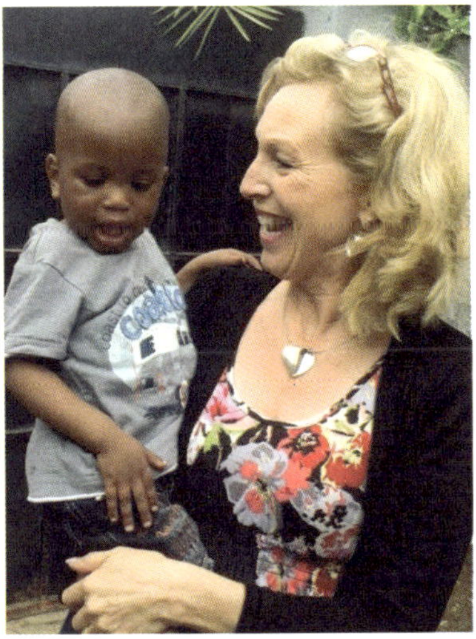

I'm grateful for those who give, those who go, and those who are on the ground working with the children. This work wouldn't be possible without the contribution of everyone.

Lawrence's Story

One young boy named Lawrence was not only rescued, but his life was changed because many people were moved by compassion to help. Lawrence was a victim of attempted murder by a family member. He had been doused with fuel and set on fire, and he used his own hands to put out the fire on his face. His fingers fused together because of the heat.

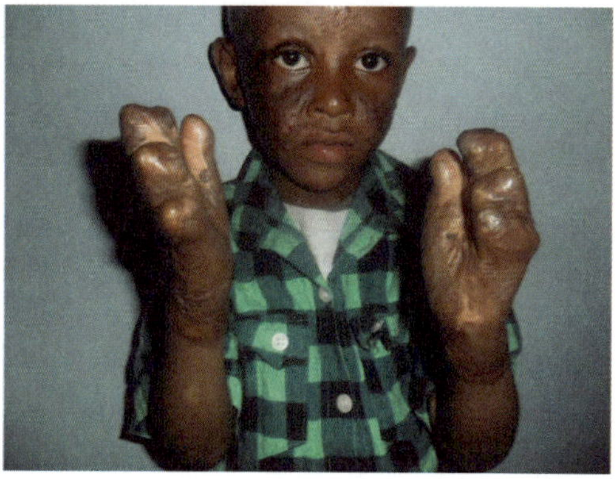

George said, "It was so sad. He must have been in so much pain. He was in the hospital for six months. The medical staff tried their best, but they couldn't help with his fingers that had fused together. He also lost the tips of his fingers in the tragedy."

A businessman who came with one of the Canadian teams met Lawrence and wanted to help him. In consultation with doctors in Nairobi and Canada, we learned that his fingers could be separated. Lawrence was living with his mother, but they were very poor, and the surgery would cost more than his mother would ever be able to pay since the average salary at the time was $1 a day. This generous sponsor paid for Lawrence to have surgery on his hands in 2013.

Lawrence can now use his hands! When he wrote with a pen for the first time, he was so excited. He has a new confidence in school, and he loves shaking everyone's hands.

My daughter Karissa was involved with the administrative work behind Lawrence's surgery. She had the privilege of visiting him in Nairobi. Here is her story of that trip.

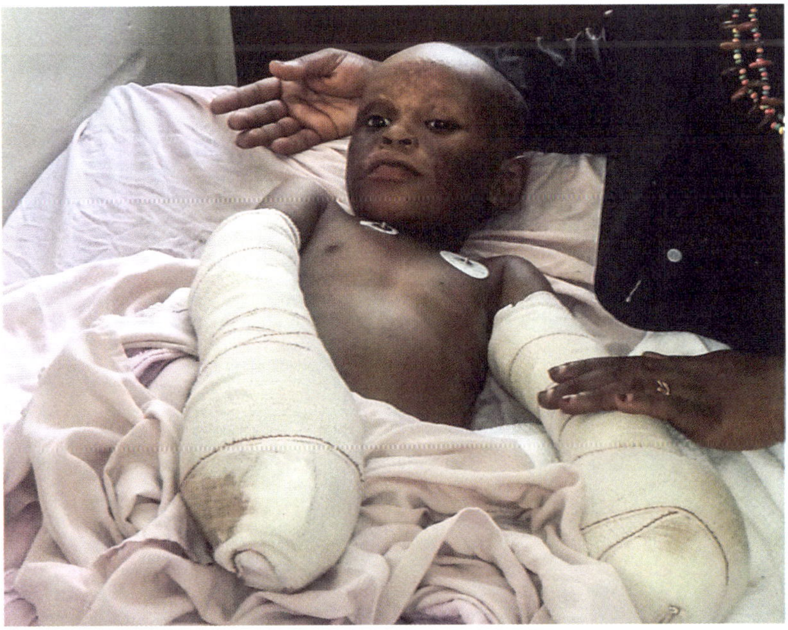

Lawrence recovering after his surgery.

KARISSA: *This moment was impactful for me personally because I had seen the photos of Lawrence. I knew his story. I was messaging back and forth with the business man helping him with his surgery, and I completed the wire transfer for the surgery.*

When I saw Lawrence in person, right in front of me, it was surreal. I had flown thousands of miles to deliver a gift to this boy from his sponsors. I read him the letter from his sponsors. I smiled at him and hugged him. He was incredibly proud of his hands, and he showed them off to me and held out his hand for me to shake. They were very soft hands, and I could see the trauma on them, but his face didn't match the trauma. He was just a bright-eyed, innocent little boy with hope sparkling in his eyes.

When we had to leave for the day, Lawrence was standing alone by our vehicle, waiting to shake my hand again. As I got closer, he put his hand out for me with a big smile plastered on his face, and I smiled right back as we shook hands one more time. This moment is etched in my memory forever.

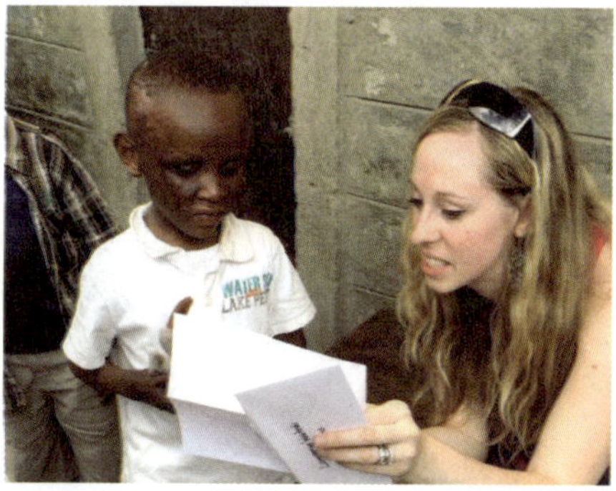

I hope to see this special little boy again! I will tell him that he is so special and brave. I will tell him that he is loved. I will tell him that his story impacts many people, more than he could ever know. And I will tell him he is **Meant 4 More**.

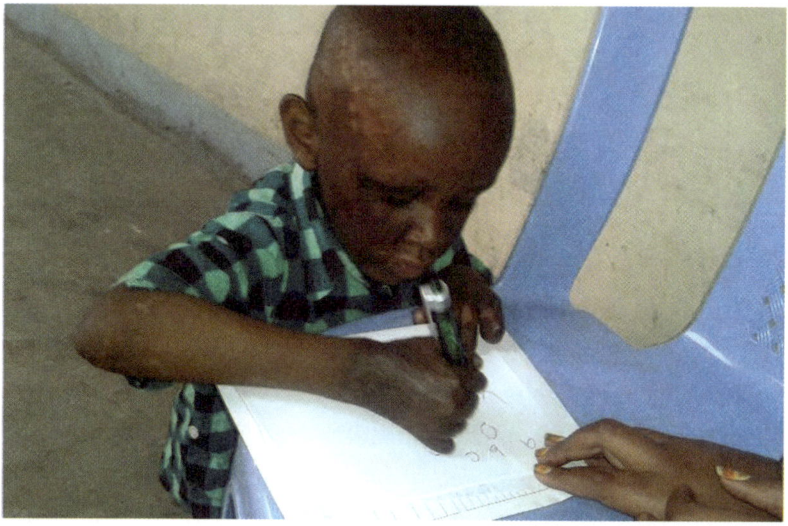

Lawrence proudly writing a thank you letter to his sponsor.

Dream Centre Today

A few years ago, Home Church in Red Deer took up a compassion offering at our yearly summer camp conference and raised money to buy land and build a beautiful building to house the Dream Centre. In February 2016, we officially opened the facility pictured below. I am so grateful for our team of caregivers whose hearts for children and faithfulness to the work has made all the difference.

The government of Kenya has been taking steps to address the tragic problem of abandoned babies, although there is a long way to go. Kenya has made maternity services free of charge for pregnant women, dramatically reducing the number of babies being thrown away in the dump. The majority of the babies now received at the Dream Centre have been abandoned at the hospital or in the slums.

The Dream Centre has a good relationship with the Department of Children's Services in Nairobi, and our center has been commended and recommended for the services we provide. We are so proud of our team in Kenya. They are doing an amazing job!

The Dream Centre location in Nairobi today.

9. TEN THOUSAND CHILDREN

It was June, 2011. We were sponsoring 862 children, and we were maxed out. Life was happening at a fast pace. I was traveling to Kenya and Rwanda several times a year, planning our ministry teams, and finding ways to help more children. Even with Karissa's help, the administration load was becoming more and more difficult.

Then something happened that I did *not* see coming.

The Next Chapter

One day I was having lunch with a Home of Hope sponsor, and he asked me about my personal life. I happened to mention to him that at age sixteen, I gave my life to Jesus. After graduating from Bible college, I was on staff with the Home Church team as a pastor for sixteen years. Then, I spent another sixteen years traveling the world, holding crusades, planting Home Churches, and now working with Home of Hope to serve children.

I paused, then said, "I just noticed that the number 16 has played a key role in my life!"

It was a significant moment. It felt like an epiphany to me. After lunch was over, I went back to the church. I wanted to spend some time praying about the significance of the number 16 in my life. I went into the empty auditorium and kneeled at the altar to pray. I started talking to the Lord, replaying the 16 – 16 – 16 pattern, and then I said, "Lord, I have been traveling for sixteen years now. Is there something more You want to say to me?"

God interrupted me in the middle of my prayer. I heard Him say so clearly, "Help 10,000 children."

I was stunned. Speechless, actually. Helping 862 children was already so much work: organizing and leading trips, finding sponsors, getting credit card information, wiring the money overseas, plus all the work involved in administration and financial accountability.

I knew that helping 10,000 children would be a huge job. Unimaginably huge. I stood up and left the auditorium. I didn't tell anyone what happened, not even my wife, because I didn't like what God had told me at all! You would think that it would be exciting to hear from God, but I wasn't too thrilled about this encounter. I tried to brush it off and forget about it.

> GOD INTERRUPTED ME IN THE MIDDLE OF MY PRAYER. I HEARD HIM SAY SO CLEARLY, "HELP 10,000 CHILDREN."

I remembered how Mary, the mother of Jesus, responded after the angel visited her and announced that she would give birth to the Messiah. "But Mary treasured up all these things and pondered them in her heart" (Luke 2:19 NIV). I kept what God had said in my heart for a few days, wondering if this could be possible and how I should respond.

I was asked to speak in my local church the next Sunday. I shared about how Jesus always asked for God's will for a situation before He did it. Jesus never did anything without first getting counsel from His Heavenly Father. He said, "I tell you the truth, the Son can do nothing by himself. He does only what he sees the Father doing. Whatever the Father does, the Son also does" (John 5:18 NLT).

If Jesus, the Son of God, did not do anything significant by Himself, why do we think we can? We desperately need to seek His face and ask for His direction. As I spoke those words, I remembered what the Lord told me earlier that week, and I immediately felt convicted.

I paused in the middle of my message and said, "I have to be honest with you. This week, the Lord told me to do something, and I didn't like it. It was a hard challenge. The Lord asked me to help 10,000 children with Home of Hope."

I remember looking at my wife in the front row. She was shocked about this big number, and she looked puzzled that I had never mentioned it to her. There I was, declaring it on stage in front of hundreds of people. We always talk and pray about such things together. Later, I confessed to her how resistant I had been and how I didn't like that direction from God at all!

I was convicted by my own message, though. (I hate it when that happens!) I repented to God and said, "Okay, Lord, I am not sure how this could ever happen—I don't want my will, though, but Your will to be done."

As it turns out, God was launching me into a new chapter of my life.

You Feed Them

Shortly after that Sunday message, I gathered some of our Home of Hope advisors, and we began to have many discussions and prayer meetings about what it might look like to help 10,000 kids. My sister Florence heard about the challenge God had spoken to me. She called me up and said, "Brian, how are you going to reach 10,000 kids?"

I replied, "I don't have a clue!"

Florence offered to volunteer more of her time, and over the years, she has given countless hours. She is always there to help in any way she can. Having gifted administrators on the team is so important, and Florence's willingness to help, along with many others who offered to help in various ways, was vital in taking Home of Hope to a new level of influence and effectiveness.

It didn't happen overnight, though! On my next trip, I remember seeing many desperate children. I looked at them all and began to pray, "God, how can I help these children? We work very hard just to help a few hundred children, but I see thousands."

I felt the Lord say simply, "You feed them."

I realized at that moment that God wanted me to raise money and feed thousands of children as part of the goal of helping 10,000 children. The phrase He put in my heart comes from the story of Jesus feeding the multitude, found in Luke 9:10-13 (NIV).

> When the apostles returned, they told Jesus everything they had done. Then he slipped quietly away with them toward the town of Bethsaida. But the crowds found out where he was going, and they followed him. He welcomed them and taught them about the Kingdom of God, and he healed those who were sick.
>
> Late in the afternoon, the twelve disciples came to him and said, "Send the crowds away to the nearby villages and farms, so they can find food and lodging for the night. There is nothing to eat here in this remote place."
>
> But Jesus said, "You feed them."

Jesus asked his disciples to feed the people even though they didn't have enough money with them. They were in the wilderness, and there was no way to buy food even if they had enough money. Yet, Jesus expected the disciples to feed them.

Jesus approached every situation knowing all the resources of Heaven were available to Him to meet the needs of people. That truth has been so encouraging to me over the years!

The Bible says that God already knows all our needs, and He will give us everything we lack if we seek His Kingdom first (Matthew 6:25-34). I don't like praying prayers for myself. Why pray that God will give me food and clothing or help me pay my bills when He has promised that He already knows my needs? I would rather pray for others! And I can have more faith that He will supply the miracles I need when my heart is dedicated to helping thousands of children. My favorite prayers are always about others.

We patterned the feeding program around the story of Jesus feeding the multitude. I mentioned this earlier, but notice the three things Jesus did in Luke 9: Jesus *taught* the people. Jesus *healed* the people. Jesus *fed* the people.

He didn't just meet their spiritual needs, and He didn't just meet their physical needs. He did both. He showed God's love in every way He could. And He did so using the unlimited resources of Heaven.

I met with our national leaders and workers in Rwanda, and I told them that I felt like God had said we needed to start feeding many more children. How could we do it? We wanted to come up with a plan for each church to serve a hot meal once per week to 100 children within walking distance of their location.

> JESUS TAUGHT THE PEOPLE.
> JESUS HEALED THE PEOPLE.
> JESUS FED THE PEOPLE.

I told the team of pastors, "If you can raise money locally to *try* to feed twenty children in your area, I will *try* to raise money in Canada to feed eighty children."

The cost to provide a child with a hot, healthy meal worked out to about one Canadian dollar. The pastors of each area went to the local leaders, business people, and even the ladies selling bananas on the side of the road. They would say something like this: "I love the children in our community. Some of them are orphans, some are living with their sick grandmothers, some children have a sick mother with HIV/AIDS. Would you consider giving one dollar a week to provide one meal, and a sponsor will match it four times over?"

The plan worked! Local people donated a little money or whatever they had to contribute, such as rice and other food supplies. The donors often wanted to go see all the kids being fed on Saturdays. Many of these people who donated became Christians and joined the church. That was an unexpected result!

> WE ALL HAVE AN OPPORTUNITY TO SERVE THOSE AROUND US. AND WHEN WE DO, IT'S AS IF WE WERE SERVING JESUS.

I often think about Matthew 25:35-40 (NLT).

> When you do it to the least of these, you do it to me. For I was hungry, and you fed me. I was thirsty, and you gave me a drink. I was a stranger, and you invited me into your home. I was naked, and you gave me clothing. I was sick, and you cared for me. I was in prison, and you visited me. Then these righteous ones will reply, 'Lord, when did we ever see you hungry and feed you? Or thirsty and give you something to drink? Or a stranger and show you hospitality? Or naked and give you clothing? When did we ever see you sick or in prison and visit you?' And the King will say, 'I tell you the truth, when you did it to one of the least of these my brothers and sisters, you were doing it to me!'

We all have an opportunity to serve those around us. And when we do, it's as if we were serving Jesus Himself. What would our world look like if we all determined to help those within our reach, no matter who they are? What would happen if we followed Jesus' example by meeting needs using the resources of Heaven?

Remember, "the least of these" doesn't mean people are less important. It means they are less visible, less represented, less powerful, less able to protect and provide for themselves. I encourage you to take a moment and ask yourself this: Who can I help? Who can I pray for? Who can I serve? Who can I feed?

Fifteen Miles for Food

The feeding program we started in those churches continues today, and it is a beautiful thing to see.

Many local church ladies volunteer, coming early on Saturday mornings to light a fire, build up stones around the fire, and begin boiling water in huge metal pots. It takes a long time to boil the water and cook the rice. There are also pots of vegetables and beans to provide protein for the children.

Some of the kids walk ten to fifteen miles one way to come to the church and receive a meal. While the food is cooking, which usually takes an hour or two, leaders sing songs about Jesus and teach Bible stories.

The team members who have accompanied us love helping with the feeding programs. They arrive early and work with the local ladies to cut the vegetables and prepare the rice. Others on the

team assist in teaching the children. When the food is ready, we form a bucket brigade line, passing plates along to the children who wait excitedly and semi-patiently for their food.

Lynzee Berreth, the operations manager of Home of Hope, had a profoundly impacting experience at a feeding program on one of her visits to our international projects. I'll let her share the story in her own words.

> **LYNZEE:** *I remember hearing about the feeding projects for the first time in a presentation that Pastor Brian gave while he was teaching at Home Church Bible College. Two of the statements that stood out were that for most of these kids, it was their only hot meal that week, and some of them would walk miles just to receive a meal. It really touched my heart.*
>
> *May 9, 2018, was the day that everything changed, and I realized why this project so touched my heart. Our team was*

in a rural village in Rwanda called Cyuru. As we were touring the property, we walked into a room and saw a giant bowl of rice cooked and ready to go for the feeding program. As I stared at it, I unexpectedly started to ugly cry! I was sobbing. I rushed out of the room to try to pull myself together. I kept telling myself, "It's just rice. Stop it. No one cries over rice."

Pastor Brian and some of the other team members turned to me, concerned. I started to say, "It's a bowl of rice," but I started sobbing again! The team was so confused about why a giant bowl of rice would make someone cry that hard.

Later that day, when I could speak, I explained to the team that I could relate so much to these children. I remembered what it was like to go to bed hungry, not knowing when I would eat next or where it would come from. My parents had separated when I was in my teens, and they each had struggles they were dealing with. Ultimately, that meant I was left alone. At age seventeen, I was homeless, living out of my car.

I knew that the bowl of rice was hope for these children! For the rest of the trip, anytime we helped with another feeding program (which we did almost everywhere we went), I would start crying again. It became the joke of the trip. We would always meet at supper to debrief about the day, and the team would say, "Well, Lynzee cried again today."

I feel so blessed to be a part of something bigger than myself that is changing lives—even something as simple as a hot meal.

Currently, we are feeding almost 5,000 children a hot, healthy meal every week. This number still blows my mind. I am so thankful for the generous sponsors who are literally giving children life with this weekly meal.

Seven Ways to Help Children

Since the early days of sponsoring 200 children, Home of Hope has expanded in many ways to fulfill the vision to help 10,000 children. Our goal is to help desperate children in the best way possible. We constantly evaluate our projects to make sure we are being effective. Over the years, our teams have come up with many innovative strategies. There are seven main ways we serve children and families.

1. Monthly Sponsorship

For rescued babies, children in need, and orphans.

2. Feeding Projects

A hot meal to help desperate and malnourished children.

3. Animal Projects

Goats, pigs, rabbits, chickens, cows, and bees to help people become self-sufficient.

4. Shoe Projects

Shoes for children, many of whom have never owned a pair before.

5. Medical Projects

Health cards for access to free medicine for twelve months.

6. Microloan Projects

Small business loans, co-ops, food carts, and other ideas to help mothers become self-sufficient and provide for their children.

7. Schools

Education is key, and we emphasize training and preparing children for the future.

I'm happy to report that by 2017, we reached our goal of helping 10,000 children! We have come so far since I visited that tiny mud hut and met four desperate children in December 2006. When God challenged me to step into this new chapter, it seemed so impossible and overwhelming. But more and more people came alongside us to reach this goal. We have truly seen the resources of Heaven at our disposal, and it is our joy and privilege to serve people—and Jesus—in these seven ways.

10,000 CHILDREN GOAL REACHED IN 2017!

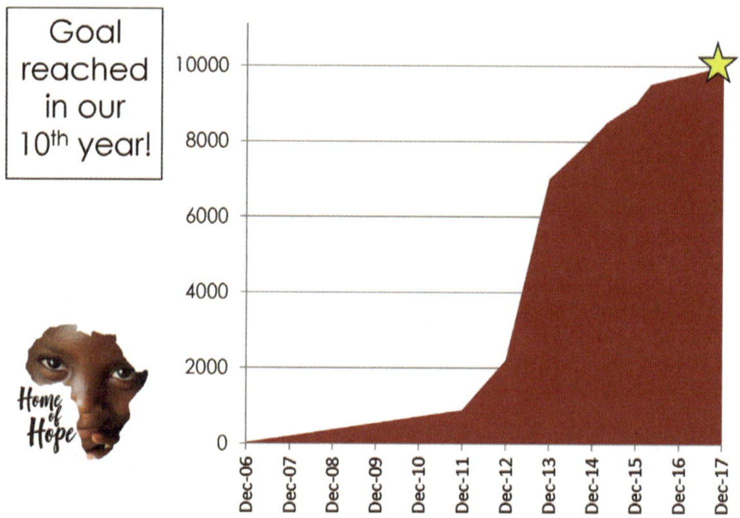

If you'd like to help in some of these seven areas, there are many ways to get involved. You can find more information at the end of this book or by visiting our website, www.homeofhope.ca. On the next page is a sample "shopping list," as we call it, just to give you an idea of how far donations go in providing tangible relief for children in need. Please note that prices might vary since the printing of this book as well as from country to country. Our website has more up-to-date information.

HOW CAN I MAKE AN **IMPACT?**

$1	Plate of Food for 1 Child Hot meal for a malnourished child.
$6	Health Card Access to medical care for 1 year.
$10	Rabbit or Chicken
$40	Pig (or Pregnant Pig $140)
$50	Goat (or Pregnant Goat $100)
$125	Microloan for a Mother Recycles every 6 months, any amount is welcome.
$475	Calf (or Dairy Cow $600) A cow would bring in $120/month income from selling the milk alone!
$500	Food Cart Help a single mother make $5-$15 a day to provide for her family.
$750	Tumaini Project - Women in Crisis Help mothers and her children move out of the slum with a microloan.
$1500	Microloan Co-ops Helps a group of 10 women for 6 months become self-sustaining.
$____	Other Present Needs

HOMEOFHOPE.CA
403-343-6570 EXT 6

* Any donation over $15 you will receive a tax-receipt.
* Amounts may vary by country.

What About You?

God can move in your life in any way He wants, of course. You may not discover that your chapters are divided into sixteen-year segments like I did, but if you take a moment to think back over the years, you can likely identify those "new chapter" moments where God led you into different and greater ways of serving others.

What is next? Remember, you are **Meant 4 More**. You can hear from Him about the next chapter of your life. He wants to speak to you! Jesus gave us the wonderful promise that all His sheep hear and know His voice (John 10:27). Ask God what He has in store for you, then listen. It is important to seek Him first in every area. The prophet Jeremiah said, "You will seek me and find me when you seek me with all your heart" (Jeremiah 29:13 NIV).

10. SERVING IN THE SLUMS

Nairobi, Kenya

OUR HEARTS WERE MOVED BY COMPASSION to meet urgent needs, but true change meant addressing the underlying issues that were creating the need. Why were mothers throwing away their babies? Why were children abandoned? And what was the best way to help?

In many cases, the extreme poverty and the lack of education, job training, and work opportunities had created overwhelming despair. They had no hope, no options, no way out. People were just trying to survive, which led them to make terrible choices that no human should have to make. The slums of Nairobi are not like the rest of the city or country. They are hopeless, dark, and desperate. Bono from U2 is quoted as saying, "Where you live should not determine whether you live or whether you die." Children born in the slum did not choose that life.

So, while we were rescuing the children who were abandoned, we also began looking for ways to give people hope and opportunities. Much of what we do focuses on helping women and children receive what they need to thrive on their own. That is why we emphasize education and microloans, among other strategies. We have seen so many positive results from giving people the tools they need to succeed!

When I found out that babies were being thrown away, I decided that we must do something. I asked our local team to start exploring more about it. As we researched, we found out that the baby problem was much bigger than the news report. The dump and the slums had many sex workers, single mothers, and teenage girls in the area. The women would do anything for some food, and they were discarding their unwanted babies. This was happening a lot. I knew we had to do something to help these women, not just the babies. In consultation with various business people who are sponsors with Home of Hope, we came up with the idea to start business training classes to help women find solutions to making money in better ways.

Into the Slums

The garbage dump where babies were being thrown away is located near a large slum called the Korogocho slum. This slum and others like it are crowded, dirty, and dangerous. We have spoken to many police officers who never go there. Those who do go in always take at least one other officer with them, carrying guns. George and the members of his rescue team risk their lives to go into the slums. On occasion, they have been attacked by criminals who assume they must have money because they rescue babies. One of his team members, for example, was attacked by men with machetes and had his arm cut badly. The thieves took his phone, his watch, and money from his pocket. Another time, George got a call to go into the slum for a rescue, but as he was preparing to leave, he received a call from a friend saying, "Don't come to the slum today! It's a trap. They want to kill you!"

I never hear the team complain. They have experienced great risk and death threats, especially when the illegal abortion clinics in the area began closing because of a lack of business. Women see our signposts and call us for help. We believe that has been instrumental in causing some nearby abortion clinics to close!

Despite the constant threats, our team still goes out to help. However, they are as wise as possible in every situation. Generous sponsors have given regular funds for the team to hire bodyguards to go with them to rescue babies and respond to emergency phone calls.

The team has told me, "What we are doing is serious work, and it is worth laying our lives down. We know that with great rescues, there is often opposition and attack. We also pray a lot and ask God and His angels to keep us safe. We will not stop."

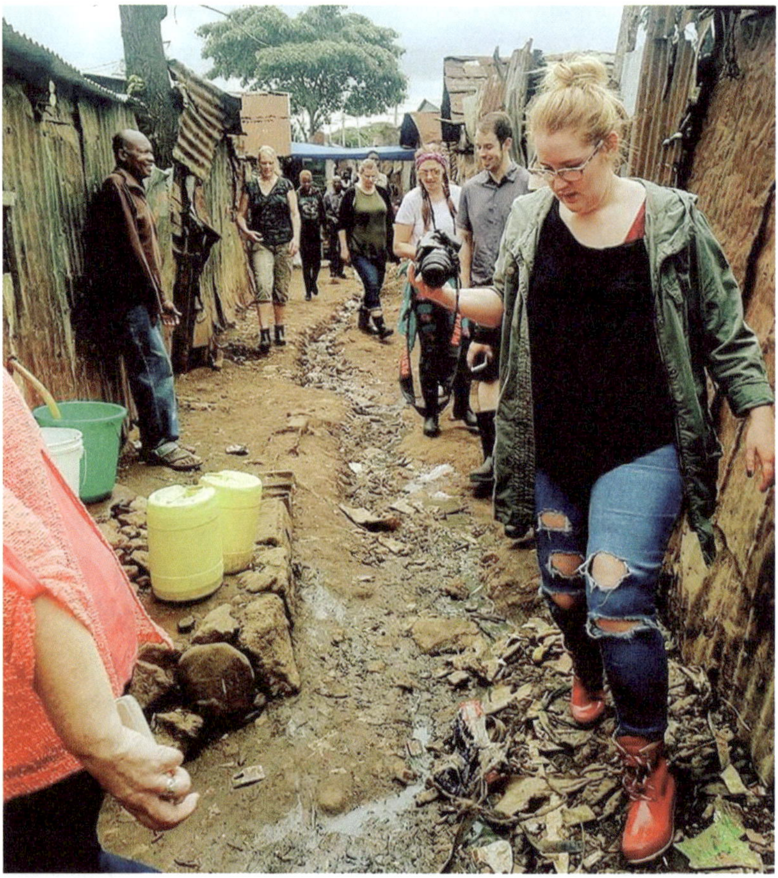

When we take trips to Nairobi, we often go on a quick tour (accompanied by two police officers) a short way into the slum so people can see where many of the babies were found.

Walking through the narrow pathways can be quite hazardous. Once, I was stepping from stone to stone, and I slipped. My entire foot went into the little sewer stream, right up to my ankle. I couldn't do anything but keep walking (with my shoe sloshing) and finish the tour. I was planning to throw the shoes away because they were an old pair I had brought for the tour, but the local team encouraged me to give them away because they were better than the shoes many people in the slums were wearing.

On one trip, we met a lady who greeted us and invited us into her little shanty. I had to bend low to get through the doorway. It was so dark inside that I had to turn my cell phone flashlight on just to see. When I did, six little children, all huddled together, were staring back at me. The "house" measured about eight by six feet. I looked up and saw countless holes in the tin roof. The floor was packed dirt with a blanket on it, and half of the floor had turned to mud from the rain the night before.

I asked, "Where did you sleep last night?" She told me that they all slept together on the dirty blanket. A mother and six children had to share one blanket in this tiny shanty! I was appalled that they were sleeping in the mud.

We gave the children some small gifts. As we left the house, I asked the team to step aside so that we could talk about it together. We had to do something to help this lady.

We brainstormed for a few moments, then we asked the lady if there was some way that she could be making money. She answered that she liked cooking and was good at it. She had a friend who sold food on the street. If she had some pots and pans, she could cook food, and her friend could sell it.

We asked how much it would cost to rent an apartment a few blocks away, outside of the slum. We were told it was only $50 per month. For someone making less than $1 a day, the average salary at the time, $50 a month was impossible.

We came up with a plan. We would give the woman $50 a month for one year (a total of $600), which would be paid directly to a landlord, plus $150 to buy pots, pans, and materials to start cooking. With this plan, she could make money for her children, and in a few weeks, she would be able to buy them clothes and send them to school.

We were hopeful that this $750 would change this family forever by moving them out of the slum and giving them the means to become self-sustaining. The rescue team responded quickly. They helped her move out of the slum and start her business *before our team even left*! It was truly beautiful.

The Best Way to Help a Child

I am convinced that the best way to help a child is to help their mother. On every trip I take, I want to give people practical teaching and guidance to live in greater financial freedom. Jeremiah 29:11 tells us that God has plans to prosper us. What a powerful promise!

Once I was teaching approximately 100 women who all lived in the slum. I asked them, "What are some of the ways you would describe the slum? What are the worst things about living in the slum?" On the chalkboard, I started to list all the things they hated about living in the slum.

- The terrible smell
- Scrap-metal shanties with holes in the roof that don't keep out rain
- Sleeping on the cold ground, which often becomes muddy when it rains
- Sickness
- Hunger and poverty
- Continual fear of violence and of being robbed
- Sewage running down the streets
- Starving people everywhere and kids crying with hunger
- The toxic stream flowing through the slum and the dump
- The 30-acre dump right beside the slum
- Very few ways to make money. Some ladies washed clothes for $1 a day but could go for days with no work. Many would go to the dump to gather plastic bags. They had to gather and wash 1,000 of them to make 75 cents.
- The hopeless feeling that they will never be able to leave the slum. "We were born here, and we will die here," they said.
- Living with no running water and no electricity
- A terrible common outhouse (which is simply a hut with a hole in the ground)

Then one woman stood up and said that all these things are terrible, but the worst is the fear of sexual assault, the fear of a man coming into their little shanty and violating their teenage daughter in front of them.

What could any of us from Canada say to these discouraged women? We did our best to love them, pray for them, and share biblical principles of finance and God's blessing with them. We pointed them to Jesus and to scriptures like Psalm 40:1-3.

> I waited patiently for the Lord; And He inclined to me and heard my cry. He also brought me up out of a horrible pit, out of the miry clay, and set my feet upon a rock, and established my steps. He has put a new song in my mouth—Praise to our God; many will see it and fear and will trust in the Lord. (NKJV)

But we wanted to do more. When I got home after that experience, one of the first people I spoke with about my trip was Pastor Barb Carritt, who helped with the women's ministry of our church. She asked me, "Pastor Brian, how was your trip? Tell me about it."

I immediately thought of the woman with six kids. I told Barb the story of how the team helped move her out of the slum and gave her the means to start her own business. Of course, I began tearing up as I shared the details.

Pastor Barb was so inspired that this rescue initiative became the "compassion project" for our church's next women's conference. The conference raised $45,000 CAD to help more women in the slums, and many attendees began sponsoring children.

Because of that gift along with the sponsorships and other gifts toward this project, 107 women have moved out of the slums of Korogocho, Soweto, and Vumilia, and 568 children are being helped because their mothers can now work for themselves. We are so grateful to everyone who gave generously at the Home Church Women's Conference.

On one of the next trips, our team visited one of the women we had helped move out of the slum. She was living with her children in a one-bedroom apartment. I asked her, "What do you like the best about living here compared to the slum? Is it the bed you have instead of sleeping on the dirt? The clothes you are buying with money from your new business? The nice washroom and shower?"

She replied, "No, the thing we are most thankful for is that we have a door and a lock!" Most shanties had only a hanging blanket for a door.

It has been such a joy to work together as a team and come up with practical ideas to help women make enough of their own money to move out of the slums. For example, one great idea was the food carts that are loaned to the women for six months. They can make \$10 to \$20 a day with these food carts. (Remember that the average was \$1 a day in the slum.) This helps them to have an action plan to get out of the slum.

We focus on helping mothers because they are the ones who generally carry the greatest burden of raising children. Our team that works to rescue people from the Nairobi slums has never come across any single fathers raising their children.

Also, the research we have done on microloans says that 95% of microloans to women are successful when they are done right. But there is only a 40% success rate with men. For this reason, most of our microloans go to help women.

After training, the microloan enables the women to begin making money and providing for their children. The goal is for them to become self-sustaining in a matter of months.

> **JUANITA'S STORY:** *Juanita is a 27-year-old single mom living in the slum with her three children. She had her first child at the age of 17 with a man who had promised to marry her but disappeared immediately after she conceived. Her mom could not accommodate her because she had other children to care for, and the burden was already more than she could handle. Juanita entered the sex trade, and because of that, she had two more children. Through our HOH rescue program, she was empowered with a food cart and can now earn a good living and care for her children.*
>
> *We are so glad that Home of Hope is not just rescuing babies but rescuing their mothers,*

> *too, and empowering them to become self-sustaining and live with security and dignity. Thank you to so many who are joining the call to help reach many women in crisis.*

Hillary Wiebe, a former staff member in the HOH office, was in complete shock when she heard from our rescue team in Kenya that most of the people who called after seeing the sign saying, "Don't throw away your baby" were teenage girls. Many were as young as fourteen years old and were involved in prostitution or had been the victims of sexual assault or incest. Hillary was only twenty years old herself, and it hit her so hard that the stories she heard were of girls younger than she was!

It wasn't just one or two girls, either. In a matter of days, over seven pages of information about girls and their circumstances had come to our office. The magnitude of how young these girls were and how many needed help was hard to comprehend.

Hillary would cry almost daily working in the HOH office as she read the stories and saw the pictures of these young girls. It was so sad to hear the stories of their lives in the terrible slum, malnourished, illiterate, and vulnerable to sexual assault.

One day, during a meeting in the office, she saw a notification pop up on the computer screen. She said to me, "I'm sorry to interrupt, but could I check this email that just came in? It's about the teen girls."

It turned out to be an email from a sponsor who wanted to give financial assistance to many of the girls right away. The sponsor offered to pay for training for these girls to qualify for a microloan so they could make their own money and possibly choose to keep their babies. Right in the middle of our staff meeting, Hillary dropped to the floor, overwhelmed and crying in absolute joy.

We believe this sort of project is a huge success. We are not only helping babies who have been rescued, but we are also helping mothers keep and support their own babies.

Blessed, Not Cursed

In any nation, there are many different cultures and beliefs. In certain communities in Kenya, some people believe that anyone who looks at or gives birth to a baby conceived from incest will be cursed for life. This belief is one reason a mother might abandon her baby, or the child might be killed immediately after delivery. If the mother were to keep the baby, the family could reject them both out of fear of bringing this curse on the entire family.

The following story, told by Janet, is a result of this superstition. Janet is an outstanding part of the rescue ministry. She fell in love with George as he was actively risking his life to rescue babies. She has become an integral part of the ministry to the mothers.

> **WINNIE'S STORY:** *One call I will never forget was from a pregnant teenager named Winnie. Her voice sounded shaky and weak as she tried to explain her terrible situation. She had found out that she was pregnant because of incest. Should she go for an abortion or have the baby and be ostracized by her family? It was a heart-breaking decision.*
>
> *She saw our signs at the dump that say, "Don't throw away your baby," and she called the number. Our team answered her call. I met with her to give her encouragement and counsel, and she came home with me that day. She lived with us in our home, and we personally gave her money. We eventually found her a place to live, and I continued to counsel her throughout her pregnancy.*
>
> *She decided to follow my counsel and not abort the baby, but instead give birth, then give the baby up for adoption. She gave birth to a healthy baby boy, who Pastors Jachin and Rebecca Mullen sponsored. Winnie asked*

them to name him. They named him Matthew Haniel Jabali, which means Gift of God, Favor, and Strong and Mighty.

Throughout this process, my husband and I talked a lot about helping more teen moms like her because we couldn't help imagining how many more lives were being lost. And we have! So far, we have helped over 300 women, many of whom are just teenagers.

We had been praying to help women in crisis before they do something drastic out of desperation. Winnie was the first pregnancy encounter that we had, and there were many more to come. Women in need see the sign, "Don't throw away your baby," and they call us. We counsel them and share Jesus with them. We invite them to church. This work is very difficult and risky, but stories like Winnie's drive me to continue to serve as many women as I can. We are so thankful for many sponsors who have helped the mothers and their children.

Meeting Winnie started a change in me to help many

women and babies be saved. Before I met Winnie, I wanted to be an accountant and was in a bookkeeping job. But when I connected with Winnie, ministering to her changed my heart and mind. I decided not to pursue accounting anymore. I want to save lives. I want to connect with teen moms. I want to make a difference.

I feel so fulfilled in what I'm doing! I am passionate, I give my all, and I love what I do. When I am talking or counseling a mom, I know that I am in the right place and that I am helping them.

Janet shared the following story as well. It is a beautiful example of the work she is doing to help mothers in desperate situations become self-sufficient. These mothers then become an inspiration to people in similar circumstances. (*Reader discretion advised.*)

JUSTINA'S STORY: *Justina was raised by a single mother 300 miles away from Nairobi. Because she was the firstborn, she saw how her mother struggled to raise the rest of her siblings. Her mother washed people's clothes and sometimes tilled land to support her family, making $1 a day—if she could find work. When she was older, it was time for Justina to start helping to make money.*

Justina had a few friends who were involved with the sex trade, which she didn't realize at the time. The lifestyle intrigued her, and after a few months, Justina gave in and decided to earn income this way. She says: "I was so desperate for anyone and anything that would support me. I would send money home, but my mom didn't know how I was making money but was grateful for the support."

In 2011, she met a man who saw her situation and

started showing her compassion and affection and made many promises. Justina moved in with him, and together, they moved to Nairobi. After a while, Justina found out she was pregnant. When she shared the good news, he told her to abort the baby. She refused, and the partnership turned into a very abusive relationship. She was scared and sought help from neighbors. When she called home and asked her mom to take her back, her mom refused due to the extra burden her pregnancy would bring.

One day, she came across our sign and called for help. She started talking to the Home of Hope counseling staff. A nearby church member offered Justina a temporary residence, and she received physical and emotional support. She began to see that she and her baby were safe now.

In 2012, she delivered a beautiful baby boy. A Canadian donor sponsored her through Home of Hope. In honor of this, Justina's sponsor named the baby. They named him Akida Hasa Busu (which means "chief, special, kiss, peace").

But Justina's story doesn't end there. She started a

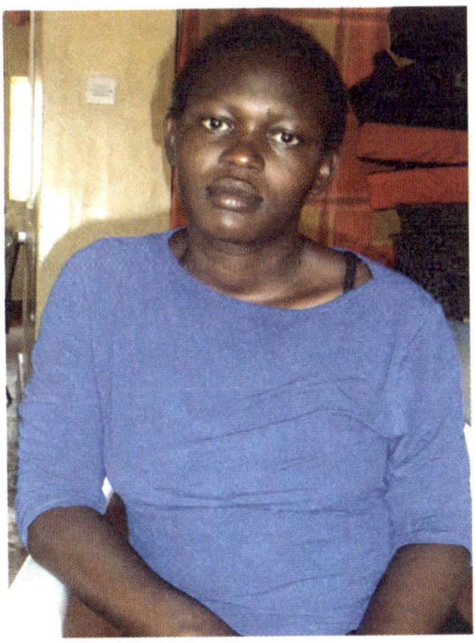

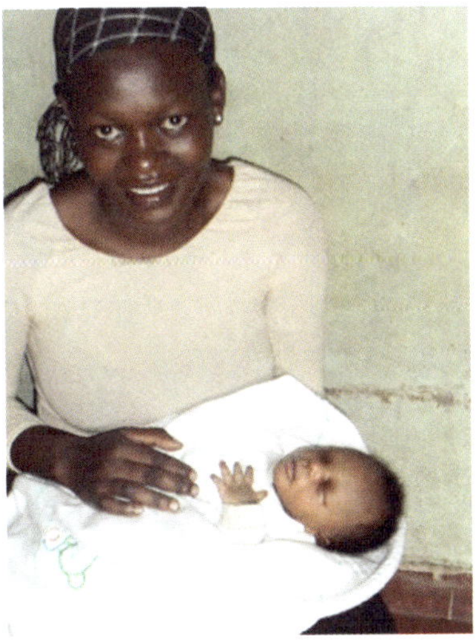

small business with a microloan. She gave her life to Christ and is committed to church. She spends her time with other young women who want to transition out of the lifestyle they are in and need assistance. Her testimony is very encouraging to these young women. Justina wants to be a good role model to other young girls. She wants to be a counselor to reach out to the many who are suffering. She has found love in her relationship with God and with the church family who love and accept her for who she was and is.

Justina is one of the women fortunate enough to escape the dangerous life of prostitution. There are many more women who remain trapped. Home of Hope needs support to reach out to more young women like Justina. This is a delightful success story. Thank you to Home of Hope and the sponsors for making stories like this one possible.

Our rescue team shared this story of a child who was born in the slum and received help from Home of Hope. (*Reader discretion advised.*)

FRANKLIN'S STORY: *When Franklin was eight months old, someone poured hot tea all over him in order to kill him. They wanted to remove all memory of him. Such cruelty!*

Franklin was in the hospital for about six months. When he came to the Dream Centre, he was malnourished. His growth was stunted, so it took a long time for him to become strong.

The picture on the left was taken about seven months after the incident. Now, years later, look at his bright smile and healed body! Thanks so much to the tremendous team of caregivers at the Dream Centre and the sponsors who helped support him monthly.

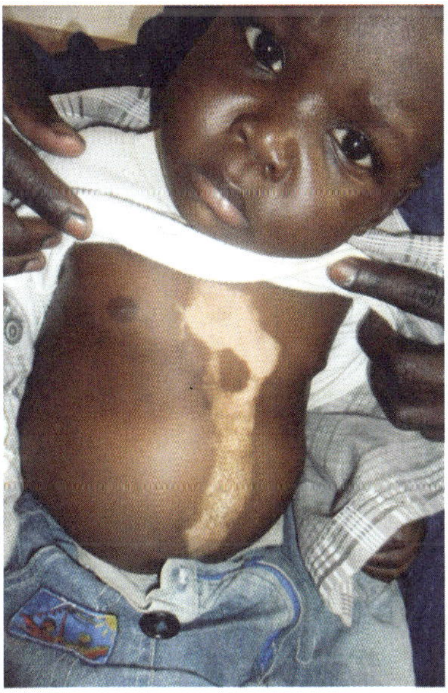

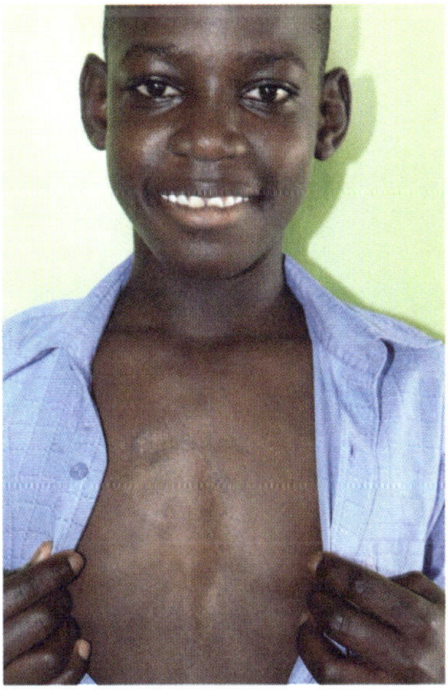

Left: Franklin soon after being rescued.
Right: Franklin today, happy and healthy.

As a team, we have been able to rescue many children and see them healed and whole. But we haven't been able to help everyone we have encountered. As hard as it is to read, we wanted to explain how it feels when these children come to the Dream Centre and the staff must fight for their survival. Remember, our team isn't seeing just pictures or videos—they are holding these children close, caring for them as they fight for their lives. (*Reader discretion advised*).

> **CONNIE:** *I have been in many counseling sessions with our leaders and caregivers. They share that one of the hardest things for them is when a baby dies. For example, they told me of twin sisters who were rescued, named Mary and Mercy. Mary is healthy and happy today. However, Mercy had HIV/AIDS and meningitis at just six months old. She went into convulsions and died because she was so weak and*

malnourished. If only we could have rescued her earlier! If only we could have helped her and her mother.

The ones who have died have greatly impacted the staff. Sometimes it is so hard for the caregivers to cope. I am glad to be on the team and able to give extra prayer and counsel through the terrible struggle of a child dying. It is such an emotional weight of responsibility. While we grieve, we are also grateful for the babies who have lived and are thriving today.

Many people in the world didn't have any concern about what was happening in Nairobi, but I'm proud of my husband for stepping up and his big heart to help. I am looking forward to future trips to train, counsel and support these front line workers who help desperate children every day.

Mary and Mercy

It is difficult situations like this that motivate us all to do all we can to reach young, pregnant teenagers who are victims of sexual assault and to help rescue their babies. All of us are passionate about helping children! We always try our best and look for the most effective ways to find them and help them. Our goal is to place these rescued children into loving Christian homes: either a foster family, an adoptive family, or a small family unit.

Helping Brings Joy

One time someone asked me, "Brian, you always seem to be so upbeat and encouraged. How do you do it?"

I replied, "I am involved in helping desperate children and poor people every day with Home of Hope activities. We live in Canada, which is a great nation. I have food. I have clothes. I have people who love me. There is so much to be thankful for! All of that helps take the focus off of my 'small' problems compared to what others could be going through."

There is something about helping other people that creates deep satisfaction. I'm not suggesting that anyone serve others for selfish reasons, but I have discovered this: helping others is the root of real joy.

Maybe you are not feeling fulfilled, you are feeling stuck, or you don't know what your passion is. In one instant, God can lead you—as He did me—into something that you can do to help others. You can try to be like the Good Samaritan everywhere you go, starting today. Don't give up! At some point, that one moment will come, and you will realize what you are called to do.

Start today by looking around you. Who can you help? What is your passion? What do you love to do?

Remember, you are **Meant 4 More**!

11. TO THE ENDS OF THE EARTH

Democratic Republic of Congo

To the west of Rwanda is the country of DR Congo. It was known for being dangerous for foreigners, especially back when we were first making contacts there. The Canadian government advised its citizens not to enter the country, and most medical insurance companies informed us they wouldn't cover our team members if we did go.

That didn't stop my good friend Elroy Pankratz. Remember, he was the one who accompanied me on my first trip to Rwanda. While our works in Rwanda, Kenya, and India were growing, Elroy connected with a pastor named Benjamin in the city of Goma, DR Congo. He visited Goma on several occasions. Elroy told me I "just had to meet" Pastor Benjamin and that I "just had to visit" DR Congo. I told Elroy that we were too busy with HOH in other countries to start in yet another country. He kept insisting, though, and about a year later, we invited Pastor Benjamin to visit us in Kigali, Rwanda. He came to Rwanda several times to see the work and receive training.

The situation in DR Congo was very difficult for women due to a high rate of sexual violence. Through the connection with Pastor Benjamin, we began helping women in Goma by giving them job and skills training and providing other support services. At first, we would bring 100 women at a time from Goma over the border into

Rwanda for the training. In 2011 we helped Pastor Benjamin launch a church in Goma, and in 2012, we started the Tumaini project in Goma, which is our ministry serving hundreds of women who are survivors of sexual assault. Tumaini means "hope" in Swahili.

I'll be honest: this is a tough chapter to write. A lot of tears have been invested in these stories and pages. As I've mentioned before, these are not just statistics or anonymous stories, but real people. We have met them, listened to them, cried with them, and served them. They are true heroes because they have overcome impossible odds.

It's helpful to hear the description of this work from the incredible leaders who head it up in Goma. Pastor Benjamin Ntahigwa (right) is our Home Church national overseer for DR Congo, and Christian Mugisho (left) is our national Home of Hope manager there.

DR CONGO TEAM: *In 2012, various searches on the Internet stated that DR Congo had one of the world's highest rates of sexual violence. One study said Eastern DR Congo was the most dangerous place for women to live. Many Congolese women have been brutally terrorized, tortured, and sexually assaulted. Most of these victims have been purposely infected with HIV/AIDS. Some of them were brutalized beyond imagination during the attacks and took months to heal from the extensive injuries. Many of these victims have been treated like modern-day lepers who are ostracized and driv-*

en out of the community to live in seclusion and rejection. They are innocent victims, yet they are openly called garbage and are rejected and disowned by their family, friends, and communities. They have no hope of getting a job or having a future; their terror will never be over.

Home of Hope (HOH) began to help women in crisis in Goma, DR Congo, in 2012 through the Tumaini Project. We provide training and support in HIV/AIDS awareness, microloans, business, sewing, handbag manufacturing, spiritual wholeness, inner healing, and physical healing. We want these single mothers to become self-sufficient with a safe place to work, live, and succeed. This project has grown to help over 1,000 violated women.

One of the first women we helped with the Tumaini Project of HOH was Charlotte, an amazing woman who accomplished so much. We first met Charlotte in 2012. She was about sixty years old and had adult children. Several years before I met Charlotte, she was the victim of a rebel gang that sexually assaulted her. Five rebel soldiers came to her house and assaulted her while forcing her husband to watch. They infected her with HIV/AIDS. They then forced her to watch as they murdered her husband. The soldiers looted her house, then destroyed it. In just a few minutes, her life, as she had known it, was over.

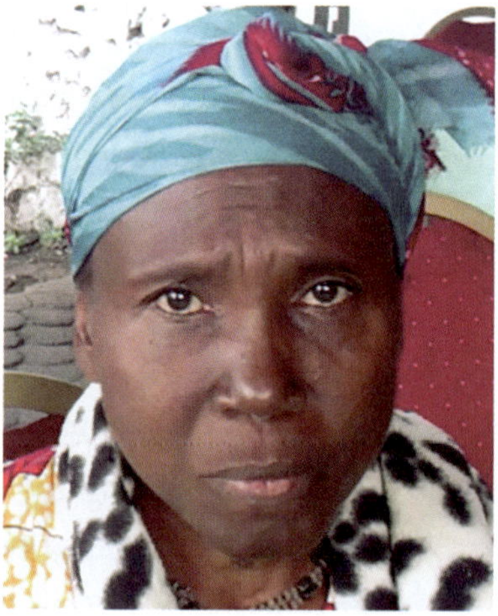

Prior to the attack, Charlotte had been a successful business-

woman who dealt in gold and other commodities. She was now homeless and HIV/AIDS positive. The inside of her body was destroyed, and she was a widow. She was ostracized from the community and called garbage. Even her adult children rejected her. And to make matters worse, the rebels bragged about what they had done to her.

Charlotte was forced to leave the community and ended up in Goma, homeless and forced to beg. She told us that the worst of it all was that there was just no hope. She had lost the will to go on.

Home of Hope started helping women like Charlotte by the hundreds. We told them about Jesus, invited them to church and Bible studies, and offered them counseling, medical help, and business training so they could start small businesses.

Charlotte's life began to change. Later, with tears flowing down her cheeks, she told us she now had hope for her future. She was so grateful for the help that she and many other women receive. She just kept repeating, "Thank you, thank you, thank you."

Sadly, Charlotte passed away several years later from HIV/AIDS. She was a great success story of someone who used her microloan to create a business that helped rebuild her life. She inspired so many others. She taught and mentored other traumatized women so they could also recover from their past and have hope for their future. She was such an inspiration!

The Tumaini Project in DR Congo is outstanding, and it is helping so many women in crisis. Home of Hope stands with these women when their own family and community won't.

Over the years, the government of the DR Congo has made an effort to deal with sexual violence against children and women. A special police force has been created, and new laws have been passed that criminalize sexual acts without consent or with minors. The DR Congo military has subdued many of the rebel groups who instigated sexual assaults, and the UN and some NGOs are also working to discourage sexual violence against women as a war weapon.

There is still a great need for healing and training for many people who have been affected by violence, especially sexual violence. And sadly, we still find many cases of abuse today. We are so grateful for those who are working for the safety of these women and children, and we are privileged to help through the Tumaini project. If you'd like to know more about this project, scan this QR code or visit www.homeofhope.ca/projects/tumaini-project.

Journey of a Lifetime

One day, during an HOH Canada advisors meeting, Elroy was telling stories from his last trip to Goma. He described what was happening there and told us yet again that we needed to visit. Dan Peters saw that I was reluctant to go at that time, so he said he would go. On his next tour to Rwanda, he traveled to Goma for a few days.

Brian and Elroy

Dan loves adventure, though, and he went further than just Goma. He was the first person on our team to get on a boat and travel to the remote Island of Idjwi (ij-wee) on Lake Kivu, DR Congo. This island reminds me of *Gilligan's Island*, an old show that you might remember: a beautiful island with no power, no water, and no modern luxuries. This is no small island, either. At 340 square kilometers, it is the second-largest lake island in the continent of Africa.

After his first trip, Dan came back to Canada and excitedly told me, "Brian, DR Congo is safe, especially this beautiful, remote island. It is such a scenic place! I am already planning my next trip to go back and to spend more time there."

Remember, this is the same Dan who once told me he never wanted to go anywhere in Africa. Now, this remote island had become his favorite place in the world! Even now, he loves to travel to strengthen the many Home Churches and HOH projects that have been established there. Just think, if Dan would have been stubborn and stuck in his ways, he would've missed out on his favorite place! After hearing Dan's stories, I had to visit.

Jesus told His followers to go into all the world to preach the Gospel: **"**But you shall receive power when the Holy Spirit has come upon you; and you shall be My witnesses both in Jerusalem, and in all Judea and Samaria, and even to the remotest part of the earth" (Acts 1:8 NASB). Other versions say "the ends of the earth" or "the uttermost places."

Whatever Bible translation you like, they all sound like a long way to travel! Idjwi Island is about as far away as you can get. I first visited in 2013. I took a car from Red Deer to the Calgary International Airport, then a nine-hour flight to Amsterdam. After a two-hour layover, I took another nine-hour flight to Kigali, Rwanda, then a four-and-a-half-hour drive in a van to the border into Goma, DR Congo. From there, we drove to the boat launch area on Lake Kivu, then we rode on a fifty-person boat (or water bus) for a couple of hours to Idjwi Island.

All of that was the easy part. Next, we rented small motorbikes. Riding motorbikes is a fun hobby of mine, but these were small 90cc bikes with bald tires and brakes that only worked when they were in the right mood.

We were planning to hold outdoor services when we arrived at our destination, a tiny village up in the hills, so we rented sound and music equipment. We had to transport all of that on motorbikes as well. One bike driver carried a guitar, his passenger held the bass drum and a stack of poles, and other bikes carried the speakers and sound mixing board. It was quite a sight!

Off we went on our six motorbikes. The dirt road was okay for a while, but then we branched off onto a narrow pathway about one foot wide, like a cow path. I tried hard to keep the bike centered on the narrow path full of huge ruts from the rain the day before. Then the smooth pathway turned into jagged rocky trails up one hill and then up another hill with extremely steep ledges.

After a two-hour motorbike off-road adventure on this remote island, the hills kept getting higher until we could not ride the bikes any further, so we started walking. We climbed over rocks and steep inclines. If you are an extreme hiker, you are probably excited to read and imagine this. I am *not* an extreme hiker.

After about fifteen minutes of climbing, we came over the crest of a hill and saw hundreds of people singing, dancing, banging on hand drums and pots, and shaking tin cans filled with rocks. They were so happy to see us. We were probably the first white people they had ever seen. Some children screamed in excitement as they ran up to us and bravely touched our white skin. Other kids screamed in fear and ran the other way.

It was quite a journey, but we had finally arrived. When the villagers finished welcoming us, I remembered Acts 1:8, which I quoted above. I looked up to heaven and said, "Well, Jesus, I obeyed! This is the most remote place I know of in the world." It was certainly the furthest I had been from home. Good thing the Bible promises us Jesus will be with us as we go to such faraway places (Matthew 28:19,20)!

I could sense Jesus' blessing and peace as I began to preach the Gospel in the outdoor landscape on this high mountain. Jesus taught many times in open-air meetings, under trees, and on mountains. Many people accepted Jesus on that trip, and a new church was started that is still going today. I am so glad I traveled all that way to tell them that they are **Meant 4 More**.

After that, we traveled to another village area for an afternoon outdoor meeting. On this sort of trip, we usually visit two or three villages per day, depending on travel and time.

We stayed at a very basic hotel on the island. There was no electricity, but the owner had solar panels that powered small lights in the corner of the ceiling area. There was no running water for washing one's hands or taking a shower. In the morning, there was a knock on the door, and they gave us a yellow four-gallon pail full of hot water to have a sponge bath. Then we hopped on our motorbikes and headed toward two more areas.

Since that first trip, the work on Idjwi Island has grown tremendously. At the time of writing this book, we are starting our fifteenth Home Church there, and we have many Home of Hope projects in place to help children and the poor.

These projects are going so well. Our feeding programs are helping hundreds of children, and we offer health cards, animal projects, shoe projects, and more (I'll describe these things in more detail later). We also have literacy classes where groups of twenty-five adults learn to read and write.

Our women's microloan co-ops are an excellent way for women

Literacy classes on Idjwi Island

to work together. For example, ten women receive ten goats, then they work to build the herd and make money together. All of these projects offer hope in the midst of great poverty on this remote island.

Yellow Water from a Ditch

One day I was riding with a vanload of people in south DR Congo. The vehicles there are always packed full. For example, if we are in an eighteen-passenger van, the pastors will keep inviting people for a van ride and crowd in twenty-five to thirty people. Apparently, it is quite a diversion to go for a van ride with Canadians!

As we drove along to our next meeting, I was shocked to notice a young boy in a ditch beside the road. He was scooping dirty, yellow water out of the ruts in the ground with a small plastic cup.

I asked the van driver to stop, but he didn't understand the English word, and he kept driving. I shouted, *"Stop!"* and slammed my hand on the side of the van to get his attention.

The interpreter translated my yell into Swahili, and the driver stopped, then backed up to where the boy was. My interpreter and I spoke with him. I had never seen anyone collecting water from a ditch to take home to his family. I was stunned!

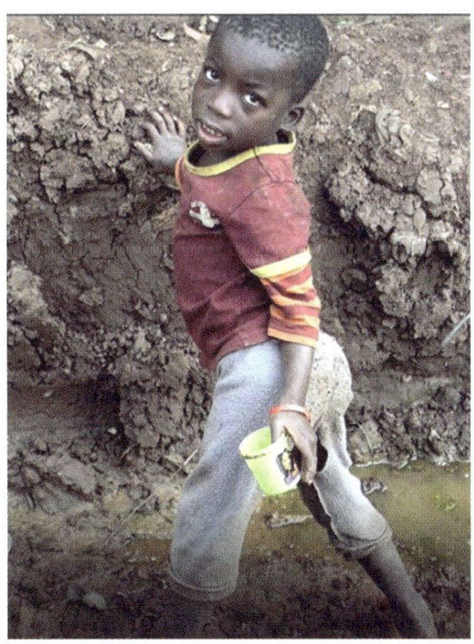

I heard the Holy Spirit say this verse to me as soon as I saw this boy: "But whoever has this world's goods, and sees his brother in need, and shuts up his heart from him, how does the love of God abide in him?" (1 John 3:17 NKJV)

In other words, if we see a need and pass by, the love of God is not in our hearts. I felt like the Holy Spirit was saying that if I kept driving and didn't help this boy, then God's love was not in my life. Wow, was I convicted!

We had some bottles of drinking water in the van, so I shared those with him. Then I asked the pastor who lived nearby to help with a little money from our fund and to find a way for the boy to get better water to drink.

That encounter was another key moment in my life where God pushed me to help more children. I cannot get the image of the boy collecting yellow water out of my mind. For me, it was a sign from God that we needed to start helping children in DR Congo.

We found out later that his name was Ahadi. He was the first child we helped in that area. I realized later that it was a test from the Lord. As we drove past the boy, the Holy Spirit stopped me and told me not to pass by, but to help him. As a result of that decision, the Lord opened the nation of DR Congo for us to help thousands upon thousands of children.

This reminds me of Jesus' story about the Good Samaritan (Luke 10:25-37). In this story, a man was beaten, robbed, and left for dead. A priest came by, but rather than helping, he crossed to the other side and hurried away. Then a temple assistant came along, but he also walked by on the other side of the road. Two people who could have helped—who *should* have helped—just passed by and kept going.

Then a Samaritan came upon the hurt man. The Jews despised the Samaritans, and the feeling was probably mutual. This Samaritan man would have been the least likely to help. And yet, he stopped to aid the injured traveler, then he went out of his way to put him on his donkey and take him to the nearest inn. He even paid the bill so the man could have time to recover.

We all need to be like the Good Samaritan *everywhere we go!* We all need to be ready at any moment for the Holy Spirit to motivate us to help someone. He wants to use us. It could be a word of encouragement, or telling someone about Jesus, or sponsoring an orphan, or getting involved with a local charity. Acts of love can change a person's life forever.

I found out years later that after we gave the boy water and drove away, he started running after our van to see where we were going. He ran and ran until he found where we stopped to have an outdoor event to help a new church. He remembers hearing my sermon that day. He said that I spoke on, "Love God, love people, love life." He started attending our Home Church and came every week for our Saturday feeding project.

Hearing this made me emotional and so thankful that we stopped to help him! On the right is an updated picture of Ahadi and our local pastor there, nine years later.

Minova Refugee Camps

As a staff here in Canada, we pray together a lot. When we hear of new areas with needs or tragic stories about children, we often spend time praying and asking God how we can help. We have learned that He will bring people and resources if we are willing to do what we can. We have seen so many miracles!

I remember one need in particular that seemed impossible. We learned of the people in the Minova refugee camps in DR Congo. People were completely stranded and had no aid at all, not even from charities or the government. There was no hope for people to leave the camps.

In our staff prayer meeting, all of us started crying as we were earnestly praying for a solution and how we could help these people. These camps were in an area with no HOH project yet, and we didn't know how to help them. We talked through possibilities and were feeling a bit hopeless ourselves. God heard our prayers, though, and great things started to happen from that prayer meeting. I will share some of them in the coming chapters. Pastor Joshua Musoka, our Minova Home of Hope leader, writes this:

> **JOSHUA:** *There are ten thousand desperate children living in the four Minova refugee camps for the last ten years. They have no assistance from the government or NGOs (non-government organizations). We are the only charity helping children there.*

I have been to this area, and I agree entirely with Joshua's statement. The refugee camps are similar to slums that I have visited. The people live in small straw "houses," which are more like straw tents. When it rains, the water goes right through the straw, and the people end up lying in the mud. Generous sponsors have donated tarps to cover many of the straw huts to keep the rain out. Many of the children are

starving. Most have no shoes, and many just have rags for clothes.

One of our granddaughters, Makayla, heard that I was buying shoes for children who have never had a pair of shoes in their lives. She was seven years old, and her birthday was coming up.

"Makayla, what do you want for your birthday?" I asked her.

She surprised me and said, "I want to buy shoes for the children you work with in Africa."

What an unexpected answer! I started crying, of course. A few weeks later, when we gave out the shoes to desperate children in the refugee camps of North DR Congo, I was very emotional. It was so impacting to tell the kids that these shoes were a gift from another child across the world who cared for them. What a great lesson for children to learn that it is indeed "More blessed to give than to receive" (Acts 20:35).

As a father of four and a grandfather of thirteen, God often uses children to speak to me. To see our granddaughter give her birthday money to buy shoes for children living in the refugee camps was beyond fulfilling. I have heard of many other children who have given their birthday or Christmas money or raised funds through work and creative ideas. Two teens, for example, started a clothing line, and they give a portion of the profits from every sale to help feed children in Rwanda. Children helping children! It doesn't get any more Christlike than that.

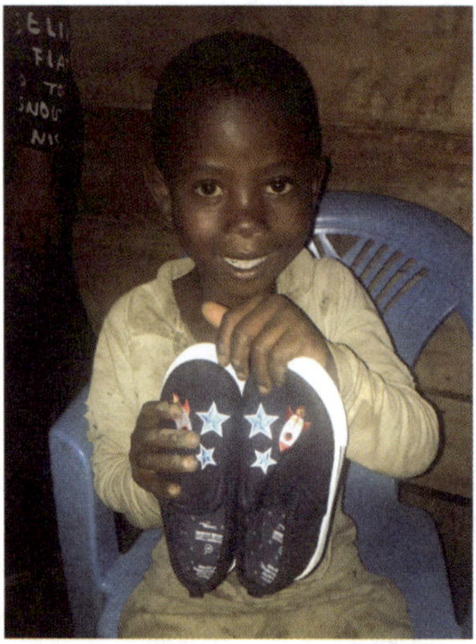

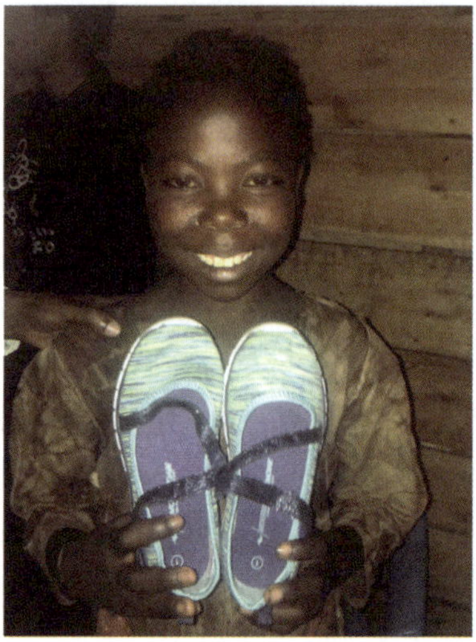

Desperate Children in Nyiragongo

Christian Mugisho has been our national Home of Hope Project Manager in DR Congo since 2015. He is married and is a father to four children. I enjoy working with him because of his heart of compassion. He has medical training and a bachelor's degree in rural development. His great skill with project management is helping his local community in a new way with Home of Hope.

Christian is a hero. He regularly makes long trips in the vast country of DR Congo to help rescue and train people to rebuild their lives. He and his growing team work very hard to help women and children in difficult situations. He has seen many children in need because he has lived in DR Congo all his life. But when he went to the Nyiragongo area for the first time, he broke down in tears. They were suffering more than any children he had ever seen. (*Reader discretion advised.*)

> **CHRISTIAN:** *I went to visit an area named Nyiragongo (near an active volcano) in DR Congo. I met 200 desperate children, many of whom were suffering from very severe malnutrition. It made me cry! At this phase of malnutrition, if not treated, children can die within fourteen days. Two of the children I had met died by the next week when I went back. This broke my heart. This is an area that is not receiving any help from NGOs or the government. They are so very desperate. They have no water because it is polluted from being so close to the volcano.*
>
> *A volunteer medical doctor went out to see these children and gave recommendations. A sponsor responded, and we started buying a daily porridge loaded with extra vitamins to give 200 of these children. The doctor said they can be saved and come back to health in six months, and they will start getting their hair back and recovering from this severe malnourishment. Also, $6 health cards can be purchased to will give children free medicine for an entire year! This is a great step that the government of DR Congo has implemented.*
>
> *Many mothers in this area can work if someone will help them get started. Sponsors have donated toward microloan co-ops so the ladies can work together to make money, like selling charcoal that people need every day to cook their food.*

As you can see, Christian has a great heart to help children in need. Along with leading our Home of Hope ministry, he sponsors a young boy named Evariste. (*Reader discretion advised.*)

> **CHRISTIAN:** *This is one of the children I met the first time I visited the volcano area. His name is Evariste, and he is only four years old. He is my first sponsored child. I donate $25 USD every month to a lady who takes care of him, and I buy him clothes and cover other needs. I see him two times a month.*
>
> 
>
> *He was born after his mother was sexually assaulted, but his mother did not love him. She got married and took this boy to her grandmother, who is blind and seventy-five years old. If nobody brought food, Evariste wouldn't eat. He had severe malnutrition at the beginning of our sponsorship, but he is recovering. He did not know his father, and now he is sure it's me. When he sees me, he wants to go with me, and that makes me cry.*

Charcoal, Food Carts, and More

Christian came up with the great idea of charcoal microloan co-ops, which have been very successful. Sometimes microloans take a lot of tedious work to oversee, but this idea has worked out well. Ten or twenty women form a co-op to sell charcoal door-to-door and in the local markets. Every day they come back to the storage shed and buy more charcoal to deliver. It is easy to keep track of with daily accounting.

Here is a picture of one of the sheds filled with charcoal. Each white sack weighs about 80 pounds, and the women carry them on their backs to deliver them to their subdivisions.

Another strategy that has worked well to help abused women is food carts. We have over 100 carts in DR Congo and Kenya. Women receive training, then we loan them these carts for six months so they can earn money and become self-sufficient.

Zuena's Story

Despite the risk, Dan Peters' wife, Evelyn, boldly accompanied Dan on a trip in 2017. Here is a story from Evelyn about someone who changed her life, a girl named Zuena.

EVELYN: *I encountered hundreds of women with similar stories on my trip to DR Congo. One that stands out is a woman named Zuena.*

Zuena is the only child of a single mom and has never known her father. When she was just thirteen, Zuena and her mother were working in a field in their village when rebel soldiers kidnapped them both, took them into the jungle, and held them as sex slaves for ten months.

When Zuena became pregnant, she was abandoned and left to starve. She spent fourteen days walking through the forest, alone and with no food. Eventually, she came to a road where she waited for two more days until she was found by a policeman who took her to a hospital in Goma, DR Congo.

The birth was very difficult. Zuena required a C-section and three blood transfusions. When she was due to leave the hospital, she had nowhere to go as she was afraid to go back to her village because of the ongoing rebel warfare in that area. Sadly, she also found out that the rebels had murdered her mother. Zuena was now all alone.

When we met her, she was scared, sad, and overwhelmed by the thought of her future in light of all she had been through. We covered the cost of a safe home for her and her baby, who she surprisingly named Evelyn after me. We gave her furnishings for her home and health care,

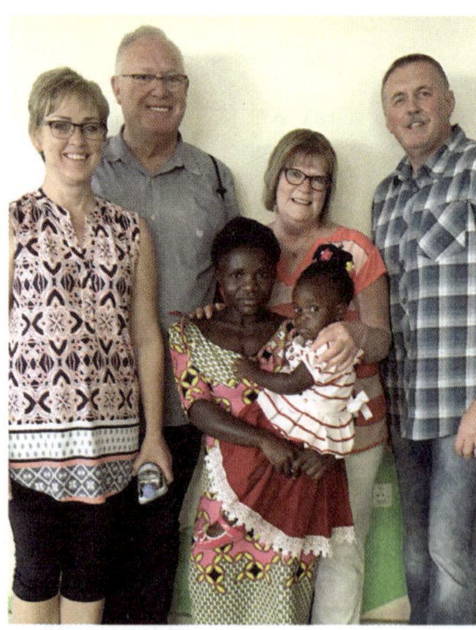

food, and some living expenses. Through Home of Hope, Zuena received training and funding to start a sewing business.

With local Home of Hope support, Zuena and baby Evelyn are healthy and building their life together. Zuena's sewing business has done very well. Using funds donated through the HOH ministry called "The Tanya Project" (named for our daughter who passed away), Zuena purchased a second sewing machine and expanded her business. She sewed the dresses she and Evelyn are wearing in the picture to the left..

The sewing projects have expanded to help dozens of women.

Sakina's Story

Imagine carrying the weight of providing for ten children as a single mother. Add to that complete rejection by your family and friends and no financial support system. What would you do? What would be the best way to help those children?

Sakina Mulamba is forty-eight years old and the mother of ten children. She is a survivor of sexual assault who tragically contracted HIV/AIDS. But she did not let that stop her from pursuing success. Sakina received a microloan from HOH to start a business to supply water to some villages around Goma, DR Congo.

One of our business people from Canada spent time with her and gave her helpful tips on how to enlarge the business to become more successful. She soon expanded her business to involve twenty other women, and from there, it grew to employ eighty other women! The women working alongside her can provide the basic needs for their families and add to their personal savings. Sakina's life is a beautiful story of God's redemption. The best way to help those ten children was to help their mother to become successful. As a result, many families received new hope and a brighter future.

They Shot Our Pastor

I communicate nearly every day with our projects around the world. The apostle Paul said the care of the churches came on him daily (see 2 Corinthians 11:28). I can relate to this feeling as I give oversight to about 100 churches. The pastors of these churches are incredible people who do so much for their communities. They face real trouble and danger.

Never was this more evident than when I received the unbelievable report that one of our pastors in a village in south DR Congo had been shot and killed. I couldn't believe what I was hearing.

"Yes, Pastor Brian," a team member told me. "A group of men with guns broke through the door of their house last night and shot our pastor. His wife begged for her life and promised some money she had hidden in the dirt floor of her mud hut. So, they let her live."

We found out that a group of pastors from the community were jealous because of the good things our church was doing. We were feeding desperate children a hot meal every Saturday. The team was also reaching out to women who had been sexually assaulted and rejected by their communities. Our pastor would tell them about the love of Jesus, and they were giving their lives to Christ. He accepted them wholeheartedly. The church was growing so much that these other pastors became jealous and hired gunmen to kill the pastor! It was so sad and difficult to believe.

As we continued to communicate about this situation, we heard that the pastor's son, Freddy, wanted to become the pastor. I asked Freddy, "Why would you want to become the pastor? If they killed your father, they will probably try to kill you, too."

Freddy said to me, "I am so proud of my father, and I want to continue what he was doing for the Lord."

Freddy decided he would sleep in various houses in the villages, staying in a different house every night, so the killers could not find him. He had eleven friends who opened their homes to him.

Eventually, the police found the gunmen, and they agreed to a lesser sentence if they revealed who paid them. Four pastors from that city are now in jail for the murder of Freddy's father.

You would think that if you wanted to feed children and help the poor, things should go smoothly, and people would be eager to help you. But there is much evil in the world, and sometimes evil people persecute and harm us for doing what is good. This is an extreme example, of course. I've never heard of another case where pastors hired hitmen to kill another pastor. But the truth is that our teams in Rwanda, Kenya,, DR Congo, and other nations put their lives at risk to help people in need. I never cease to be astonished by their commitment and courage to share the love of Jesus through their words and actions. I am so proud of our leaders. They are on the front lines, and they are doing an exceptional job.

How About You?

I am so glad I listened to my friends Elroy and Dan and that Home of Hope is now in DR Congo. Because of generous sponsors and the work of our national team, we are helping thousands and thousands of children. God used the little boy who was scooping up yellow water as the catalyst to begin helping children in one of the most difficult nations of the world.

What about you? Is God using anyone to challenge and encourage you to step out and take a risk? Are there needs or people you have been passing by, but God is asking you to stop and help? Is there someone you can reach out to with a helping, loving hand?

Let the love of God that is within you motivate you to help others. You never know what doors will open and how many lives will be changed because of your acts of generosity.

12. DON'T CHANGE THE CHANNEL

THERE IS NOTHING LIKE BEING PHYSICALLY PRESENT with someone experiencing desperate circumstances to bring home the reality of their suffering. You can't look away. You can't walk by on the other side. You can't change the channel.

And you don't want to. When you listen to someone's story, you are reminded that people matter more than anything: more than fame, more than comfort, more than riches, more than success. You understand that you can't solve all the problems they face, but you can show love. You can give as you are able, and God uses what you have to accomplish the miraculous.

It is this face-to-face connection that impacts the people who have accompanied me on trips to our projects. I have taken hundreds of people over to Rwanda, Kenya, India, DR Congo, and other nations, and they are always so moved by the experience. They meet real people and hear real stories, and they are never the same.

People are often intimidated by the idea of going to another country and culture, but anyone can do this. Remember, you are not going to change the whole world: you're going to connect with other human beings who are more like you than they are different from you. You are going to both teach and learn, give and receive, love and be loved.

In the following pages, I'd like to share a few stories from the perspective of people who have gone on trips with me. There have been many intense experiences and tragic stories along the way. We have shared a few of them in this book, but there are many more that have touched our hearts and shaped our ministry.

There have been some funny ones, too! Dan Peters—who initially didn't even want to go to Africa—seems to have a unique ability to get himself into crazy situations. He loves recounting them, and he keeps us all laughing. What is most amazing to me is his ability to face genuine hardship and discomfort with a cheerful, grateful attitude. He manages to find the humor and opportunity in each one.

For example, here is a "unique" bus ride he experienced, told from his perspective. I apologize in advance for the colorful details...

> **DAN:** *Just getting from one place to another in some areas can be an adventure all on its own. I remember one day that started with an early morning flight from Nairobi, Kenya, to Kigali, Rwanda. There I got on a 48-seater bus with 60 or more passengers plus the odd chicken. During this six-hour ride, we enjoyed some of the most gorgeous mountain forest regions I have ever seen as we traveled to Kamembe, Rwanda.*
>
> 
>
> *A couple of hours into the drive, a lady two seats down from me started making increasingly louder and louder*

groaning sounds. I thought she might be praying because the drivers tend to be very heavy-footed, and the bus was swaying back and forth as he sped around hairpin curves up and down mountainsides. The groaning intensified and was getting the attention of more passengers when suddenly the true reason for the sound became clear. Too clear. She threw up all over herself and the bags she had on her lap.

Some people started laughing, which woke the toddler in the woman's lap next to me. When the young fellow looked to see what had happened, the strawberry yogurt he had finished before his nap suddenly wanted to see the light of day as well. The lady right in front of the toddler (with the blue and white striped top) was the one who had started all the laughter. Without warning, she projectile-vomited her beans-and-rice lunch down the neck and back of the young girl in front of her. This girl turned around, horrified, and immediately threw up herself.

We had another three hours left to go, and the driver did not stop. There was nothing anyone had to clean any of it up. My role in all of this was to pretend the window was stuck open.

As I write this, I am now enjoying my supper of fresh, fried mini fish, called sambasa, with a salad and a beautiful view of Lake Kivu. Not sure my wife would have enjoyed herself on this one. Trips with Home of Hope are a blast!

A Father-Daughter Trip

Pastor John Boyes is a wonderful Home Church pastor from Sundre, Alberta. He has taken three trips to our African projects and is a very creative and interesting teacher. John is also a great father, and it is so good to have fathers come on teams to love on rescued babies and children.

The picture here is when John first met the child he and his family sponsor, Deo, and took him on an outing to the mall. The backpack is filled with toys and gifts from John's two children back in Canada.

On John's next trip to Africa, he brought along his daughter Judah-Ann. This time, Judah-Ann went with Deo on a shopping trip in downtown Kigali, Rwanda.

John said, "It was one of the greatest joys of my life to see Judah-Ann step into her ministry on our trip. It was so fulfilling to see the character and love of Jesus displayed through her! She patiently dealt with the rigors of the trip and worked to touch people's lives and connect them to the Father."

> **JUDAH-ANN:** *Going on a trip to Africa with my dad did so much for us both. It built our relationship, it built our ministry together, and it taught us both so much about joy and gratefulness. My dad and I went on our trip in 2018 when I*

was sixteen. I was excited to see other cultures and get a different perspective on telling people about Jesus.

Judah-Ann with Deo in Kigali, Rwanda.

As we traveled to different towns, my dad would teach, then I would teach. I enjoyed teaching on the trip because the hunger for the Bible was amazing. I loved my trip with my dad, and I'd highly recommend it to everyone to go with family members. It is so much fun to grow and learn together.

I also loved spending hours at the HOH Dream Centre in Nairobi. Teaching the children, singing songs, playing games, and loving these rescued children was incredible.

A highlight of my trip was when I met Samuel Lucas, a deaf and mute boy living there. Samuel and I had a special connection because I knew sign language and was able to communicate with him. He is a super bright boy! He could sign faster than any child his age I'd ever seen. We sat on the floor for hours, signing, playing, and doing his homework.

Samuel was so special because even with his disabilities, he was feeding oatmeal to the younger kids, helping clean up, and doing all he could to serve. He had found his place. It was so cool to think that because of the Dream Centre and the great caregivers, Samuel now has the opportunity to show the world what he is capable of and who he is.

Samuel's Story

Reader discretion advised

Samuel Lucas, the boy Judah-Ann met, was rescued in 2011 when he was four years old. A phone call came to the number on the signposts that say, "Don't Throw Away Your Baby." The caller said there was an abandoned boy. Perhaps the huge responsibility of raising a boy who was both deaf and unable to talk was too much for his parents, and they chose to discard him.

When George arrived at the scene, there were many people gathered around. Some were saying, "This boy will just be a burden," "No one wants him," and "He is cursed." Some even said, "He deserves to be eaten by animals or to be used as a spiritual sacrifice." How terrible! Hearing these statements, George was even more motivated to rescue him.

Usually, we rescue babies. But how could we help a boy like this? What a challenge! It was a situation that needed a miracle, but we knew he deserved to live, not die, and that he was a blessing, not a curse. Samuel Lucas was **Meant 4 More**. A loving sponsor began to support him monthly and give extra donations for him to attend a special school. Another sponsor gave money to help the caregivers learn sign language to communicate with him.

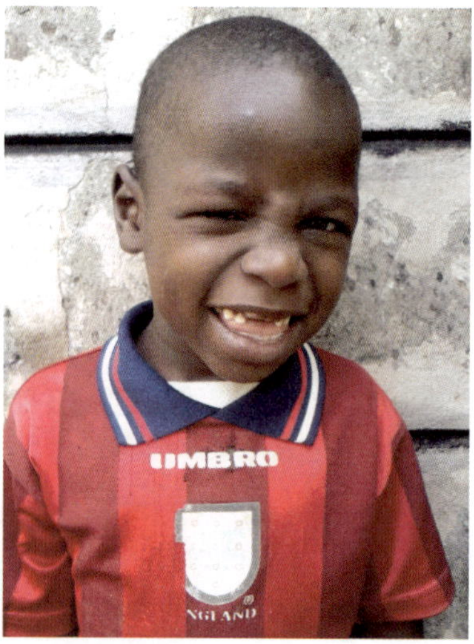

I appreciated it so much when Judah-Ann came on the team with me. She was so caring and kind to all the kids. I would be gone for the day and come back, and Judah-Ann would still be sitting on the floor with Samuel,

teaching him and talking in sign language. Someone discarded him because of his disability, but Judah-Ann reminded him of his value.

The caregivers at the Dream Centre wrote this about him. "Samuel is a very strong and mighty young man! Although he is deaf and mute, he does not let that define him. He works extra hard to learn sign language so he can communicate with his teachers, and even some of the other kids at the Dream Centre are learning so they can talk with him. He is always happy and loves to laugh and play with others. He is known for always doing his best. He has a pure and kind heart and is doing well in school. He enjoys washing dishes and clothes and doing manual chores. He wants to be a driver when he grows up."

Stories from My Family

One thing I have loved about helping children over so many years is that my entire family has wanted to be involved. Our four children and their spouses have sponsored children and traveled with me. I am so proud of all of them and their generosity. Here are some of their experiences.

OUR SON, BRAYDEN: *When Home of Hope started to rescue babies, I asked to be put on a waiting list to sponsor a baby financially. One day I received the call that a baby girl had been rescued and needed a sponsor. I asked what the baby's name was, and they said, "The baby does not have a name. Would you like to name her?"*

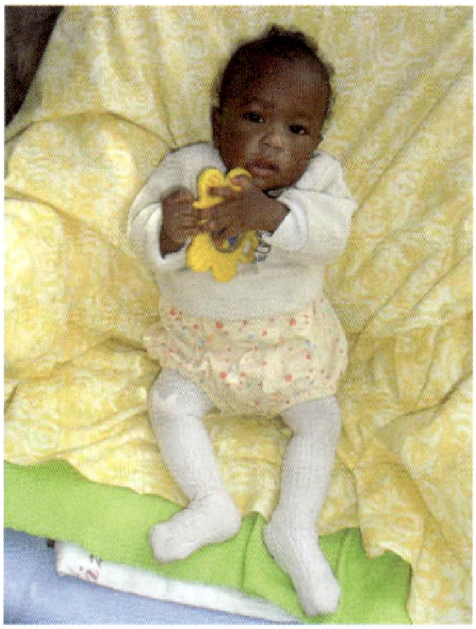

Naming a child is a huge responsibility. It's something that a child will carry with them, and it is their identity for the rest of their life! After thinking about it and researching Kenyan names, I settled on the

name Anai Avia. Anai means "heard my cry," and Avia means "God is my father." This little girl's story is one of rescue and hope, and her name is a testament to her rescue story. God literally heard her cry, and He is her father. I pray as she grows up that she remembers that she is a child of God, that He is her father, and that He listens to her every cry.

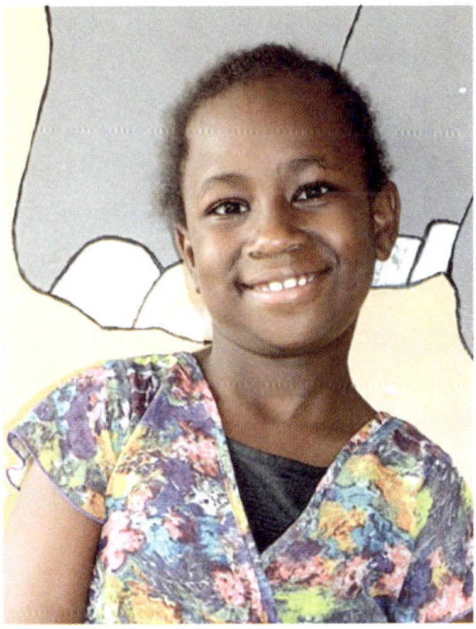

On my next trip to Kenya, I met Brayden's new sponsored child Anai—this special little girl who is now part of our Thomson family. Every time I go, I always spend time with her, take her on dates, and send Brayden lots of pictures and videos. Isn't she sweet? And she is such a leader!

My wife, Connie, has been so supportive of everything I have felt led by God to do, including all the challenges, sacrifices, steps of faith, and traveling. She rarely goes with me because she never sleeps on planes; so she arrives at her destination completely exhausted if there are long flights. Connie always jokingly rephrases Isaiah 6:8, a well-known Bible verse, this way: "Here am I, Lord. Send my husband."

I remember once, though, years ago, when I asked her, "Connie, we have been invited to speak at a marriage seminar in South Korea. Do you want to go?"

She responded, "No, I don't think so."

Then I added, "We could stop in Hawaii on the way home for only $18 more a person."

She immediately replied, "Okay, I will go!"

I said, "Don't you want to pray about it?"

She said, "I just did!"

After I had been to Rwanda a few times, I persuaded Connie to go to Africa with me a couple of times. I was so glad for her to see the things I had told her about. We traveled to the rural village of Jabana, Rwanda, visited the mud huts where sponsored children lived, and returned to our simple bed-and-breakfast hotel.

I said, "Connie, wasn't that a great day today?"

She said, "Yes, it was okay—but I don't enjoy all the dirt and dusty roads. It feels like camping. And I don't like camping!"

Although traveling was not her favorite activity, she loved the people she met. Both in Rwanda and later, on a trip to Kenya, Connie was so excited to hug the rescued children and to teach many women.

Our daughter Joy and her husband JD wanted to sponsor a child with HOH from the beginning. Joy said to me, "Dad, I really want to go with you on a trip and to meet our sponsored child, but with young children, I will wait to go until our youngest child turns three.

A few years later, Xander, their youngest, came up to me and said, "Papa, I am three years old now."

I said, "Great! Thanks for telling me."

"No," he said, "Papa, I am now *three*!"

In the background, I noticed Joy smiling, and it all clicked. Tears came to my eyes as I was so excited that Joy was planning to go on a trip with me. She is a great pastor in Leduc, Alberta, and I knew her teaching and training of women and leadership in church meetings and conferences would be a great asset.

She said, "Dad, I want to make sure I have lots of time to hug the babies who were thrown away in the dump, and I want to hug Emmanuel, our sponsored child in the Dream Centre in Nairobi, and Kellia, our sponsored child in Rwanda." Below is the story of Joy meeting Kellia for the first time.

OUR DAUGHTER, JOY: *We started sponsoring Kellia in May of 2012. She was three years old, which was special to us because we have a daughter who was the same age. We started sending letters and photos to get to know her family situation. Her father had been killed by poisoning, and her mother was sick. Kellia and her brother were starving and in a bad situation. When we started sponsoring them, their situation improved quickly as her mother also started a business with a microloan from Home of Hope.*

My husband, JD, met Kellia on his first trip to Rwanda, just a few months after we started sponsoring her. She won his heart with her friendliness and silly grin. I was home with our three young children and looked forward to the day when I would finally get to meet her.

In April of 2016, I had the privilege of going to Africa with Home of Hope. I was so grateful to see the tremendous organization my dad had started nine years earlier and to meet the people we had prayed for and invested in for

many years. Most of all, I was grateful to meet our Kellia, who was now seven years old.

The day I met Kellia, I remember pulling up to the Home Church that she attended and feeling so much anticipation to meet the little girl who had been part of our family for four years. The pastor of the church brought Kellia and her mom over to meet me, and it was such an incredible moment. As soon as she saw me, she knew who I was, and she ran right up to hug me. She held on so tightly for a couple of minutes. She looked up at me, and we both cried. I was so thankful to finally meet someone I had loved for years.

We spent the morning teaching at her church, and she was by my side, holding my hand all morning. I taught in the kids' Sunday school, and they asked such intelligent questions about God's purpose for their lives and the Holy Spirit. It all blew me away. Then after church, we were able to take her out for lunch and spend a few hours with her! It was absolutely unforgettable to feel the love that Kellia had for me and to know that we weren't just making a difference—we had made a lasting connection.

Kellia's mother was ill and weak, so she was not able to work very much. This made the sponsorship very important. Sadly, in 2020, Kellia's mother died. Kellia now lives with a fantastic church member who has a house sponsored by my sister Florence.

As Joy mentioned, her husband, JD, went on a trip with me. I have very vivid memories of JD delivering pigs. We had four motorbikes, each with a driver and a passenger who was responsible for carrying a pig. They went off to deliver the pigs to needy families.

Four hours later, JD came back, exhausted, and with his face covered with dirt from the dusty bike ride.

"Wow," he said, "See that huge hill? We went up the cow trails and over that mountain. People walk a long way in rural areas! But four needy families received a pig delivered right to the door of their mud huts."

JD is a talented sketch artist. He had the idea of drawing a picture of one of their sponsored children, Emmanuel, and sending it over with his wife Joy. Emmanuel, who was living at the Dream Centre in Nairobi, had earned the nickname "Mr. President" because of his big personality and leadership skills, even as a child. So JD drew him a picture as the future president of Kenya.

Emmanuel as the future president of Kenya.

Our oldest son, Ryan, is a fun-loving person, and any trip with him is always filled with laughter. He stands out wherever he goes because he is so tall, and of course, his light-colored skin makes him all the more obvious. Everywhere he went, young Rwandan children would smile, laugh, and shout the word "muzungu" at him. He asked what it meant, and we told him it was "white man."

He wanted to engage with the kids. So, he came up with an idea. He asked the translator, "When the kids see me, they yell, 'hey, white man.' How do I say, 'hey, black kid' in your language?"

They taught him how to say "mwirabura," which means black

Can you find Ryan in this picture?

child. So, for the rest of the trip, every time a child would say, "muzungu," he would reply, "mwirabura." That made the kids laugh so hard! They loved Ryan a lot. As you can see in the photo, kids swarmed around him everywhere he went.

Ryan has always loved cameras and video. He spent hours every day taking pictures of sponsored children and gathering materials for promotional videos so that more people could find out about HOH.

One of the things we do when we return to Canada after a trip is to debrief with the team. We go around the room, and everyone gives a highlight of the trip or something that touched their heart.

Ryan is the kind of person who doesn't cry about much, but he said, "I got a tear in the corner of my eye when we met Jadon, the little boy who was so hungry that he sucked all the skin off his fingers. Meeting him was something I will never forget." (Jadon's story is told in chapter 8.)

Ryan's wife, Sarah, also wants to come on a team. Like Joy, she is waiting until her five children (yes five!) are grown up a bit and over the age of three. We are hoping she can join us when her oldest daughter, Katelyn, is in her teens.

Of course, our daughter Karissa is very involved with the administration side of everything Home of Hope does. She has also joined us on trips, as I mentioned earlier. It was beautiful to see the pure joy on her face as she delivered gifts from sponsors for their HOH children in Nairobi! Here is Karissa's highlight.

> **KARISSA:** *Delivering Christmas gifts from a sponsor to the child is a lot more work than you'd probably imagine. We start by collecting the donations and making sure they are all labeled and inspected properly. Next, we confirm that the list is correct and given to each location, to make sure that those children will be at that place on the exact day of our trip. It is quite the undertaking! But once we have organized that location's gifts into the suitcase, traveled there, and started giving the gifts away, all of that work was worth it!*
>
> *It was even more worth it to personally deliver the gifts that we had worked hours to organize. Seeing a child's name on a sheet of paper does not compare to looking into the child's eyes and knowing that they are a real person, no different than the children in my family. They have hopes, dreams, silliness, and innocence.*
>
> *Many times, children would open a gift and later try to leave without it. It was hard for them to understand that this gift was for them. To take home. To keep. It was as if many of them had never been given anything before. I explained that someone across the world bought this gift just for them, and they could take it home.*
>
> *Since that trip, I have had two children of my own, and I have a different perspective now than I did in the picture here. I understand children better now. I can see the world through my children's eyes. I know that my next trip to Africa will be completely different because I have new eyes on the world, and I hope that I can use that to impact more people's lives.*

On one occasion, Karissa and her husband, Garrick, came on a trip with me. It was great to share the gospel together and cut the ribbon of a new Home Church that opened in west Rwanda. We would travel hours every day in a van over bumpy Rwandan roads. Often, when Rwandans would go with us, they would sing loudly and passionately as we drove. As the bumps in the road increased, our heads would be jarred, and everyone's bodies would shift and bump into each other in the van. They called it "dancing in the van."

Garrick loves to read, and he would often be reading one of his books as we were driving. He says that he read eight books on that trip. I couldn't understand how he could read so much and not get sick on the bumpy roads! Garrick enjoyed being on a trip with his mother, wife, and me. One of his key memories took place in Mugomero, Rwanda.

> **GARRICK:** *One day, after we had just delivered goats to some people in need and were on our way back, we met a little boy who was one of the saddest looking kids I've ever seen. Many children are still happy despite the circumstances they're living in. But this little boy looked truly hopeless. There was no joy and no emotion. He just seemed like a hollow shell. His clothes were practically non-existent, with more holes than cloth. He had no shoes. I had to know what his story was and how we could help him.*
>
> *We pressed the interpreter to find out more information for us and discovered that he was an orphan who had been taken in by a woman and her children. This wom-*

an, who was not his relative, only knew that he had been orphaned and had no one to take him in. She had nearly nothing to offer him but had determined that she would try her best to take care of him as well as her own children. They had been squatting, moving from place to place as they got pushed out of where they were staying with the meager belongings they could carry. They were staying in a mud hut that they had found, without any certainty of the future. They urgently needed help.

Karissa and I talked to the leader of the area, Ernest, and decided to personally buy him some clothes and shoes. We bought them a huge bag of food and a goat. The clothing and food would take care of the immediate needs, and the goat would give them the potential for recurring income for the future. This had the potential to change the rest of their lives. We left some cash with Ernest that day for him to take care of them for us. A few days later, Ernest sent receipts showing that every dollar was spent properly, and there were also pictures of the family with the gifts. Ernest did a trustworthy job in how he handled the situation.

That day we were able to show that family that they matter and that God sees them. In one day, everything can change.

Our son Brayden really wanted to go on a trip, and we decided to go together with him for his Grade 12 high school graduation present. Connie, Brayden, and a few other people were on the team with me. Brayden has always loved kids. He wanted to work in the church nursery as soon as he was allowed to as a young boy, helping in any way he could. So, being in Rwanda, surrounded by kids every day, was so fulfilling for him.

His heart went out to a little boy he saw wandering alone on a dirt road. The boy was dressed in terrible clothes and looked like he

had never had a bath. Brayden had the joy of taking the boy shopping for new clothes and rice to take back for his family.

After spending time with the boy, taking him shopping, and asking him questions, Brayden found out he lived with his grandmother. He decided to sponsor the boy every month.

After Brayden finished Home Church Bible College, he led a team of eighteen people back to Rwanda. One of the things he wanted to do on his second trip was to help make a mud hut, stomping on mud and forming the mud into bricks. He set the schedule to spend more days in each area, rather than just going to a different location every day. It was a great idea!

All four of our children and their

spouses attended Home Church Bible College. A great foundation for great marriages is being zealous for Jesus and going to Bible college—or, as I sometimes call it, "Bridal college."

Candace, Brayden's wife, went on a team with me when they were engaged. It was a great time to get to know her better. I remember coming home and Brayden asking me, "So dad, how did Candace do on the trip?"

I said that I really liked her and gave him some highlights. I added, "I noticed how she never complained." Some parts of a trip to a foreign country can be physically and emotionally demanding, but I never heard anything negative come from her mouth. So I continued, "She is a good girl, and I am happy you are going to marry her!"

Everyone Has Something to Give

I've been on many ministry trips, so I know how to look for the potential in people, and I will gently push them and support them to step out and do things they have never done before. I find joy in noticing things people are good at and then taking them on a trip and seeing them do those things to help people. I have taken all kinds of people with all sorts of talents and giftings.

Everyone who goes has something to give. I have yet to be stumped by a talent I couldn't use on one of these trips. You don't have to be a great public speaker. Maybe you are a great hugger or smiler. Maybe you have a talent you can teach others. Maybe you know how to build things or fix things. Maybe you understand finance and business. God can use whatever He has given you to bless others, and there is nothing greater than allowing yourself to be used by Him.

There is always a place on a team for someone who comes with an open heart and a willingness to serve others. For example, one of my new friends, Denis Fugère, started riding motorcycles with me.

As we talked, I found out that he was also a very handy man and could do just about anything. He and his wife Katherine came with me to Malawi, and he helped put a roof on our first Home Church building in Malawi. It turned out that he was as entertaining as he was handy. He danced and made children laugh, and he was a huge blessing on the trip.

I first met Katherine at our Home Church in Red Deer when she started sponsoring a child monthly. She fell in love with Home of Hope and began volunteering at our events. She loved the idea that she could apply to go on a Home of Hope "discovery tour" (which I'll explain in a moment) and meet her new sponsored child. Before they knew it, Katherine and Denis were preparing for their first African trip.

Just a year later, the two of them led their own team of eight people back to Africa, where they spent time serving and teaching. In addition, they are now faithful sponsors of three children through Home of Hope.

> **KATHERINE:** *The trip to Malawi changed us in very big ways. Monumentally, actually! It radically transitioned our hearts, and ultimately what took place in both Denis and me while on that trip changed the trajectory of our lives. Those changes have helped lead us to where we are today, both as individuals and as a married couple.*

Each spring, right after Bible college and university students are done their year of studies, is a great time to go on trips. I love teaching in our Bible college, training students, then leading them on an adventure. I tell them that testifying, teaching, or preaching is a lot easier in Africa than in Canada. All the beautiful faces beam with delight when a guest begins to teach. In some places we go, it is the first time they have ever seen a person with different skin color. I tell people that it is so easy to stand up and tell your story. You just start by saying, "Hi, I am from Canada," and they will loudly cheer every time.

Lynzee is a Home Church Bible College graduate, and she has been on staff with HOH for a few years. She was adamant that she had to go on the 2019 trip to DR Congo with my team. I told her that the area we were visiting could be particularly dangerous for women, but she insisted. With her mother's blessing, Lynzee signed the waiver forms, and we allowed her to come.

One day, we were doing an outdoor event. At this kind of event, we would often begin with a dance competition to gather the crowds of people. Then the team would get up and share the gospel and give testimonies. Here is what Lynzee remembers from that day. It was fantastic! All of us were amazed at what the Lord did through her.

LYNZEE: *Pastor Brian will often push us to do things we have never done. This was one of those times. In the middle of an outdoor service, he came over to me and said that he would like me to be the next to speak! I suddenly was very nervous, and I asked him what I was supposed to say to this huge group of people. He suggested that I share my favorite Bible verse, tell a Bible story, or give my testimony. Then he walked away, leaving me trembling and shaking.*

I am a preparer. I need to be prepared to feel confident in what I'm doing. This was not enough time to prepare.

As I began walking up to the stage, I couldn't remember a single Bible story or Bible verse. Blank. Nothing there. But, I knew my story because I had lived it—so I started there.

With a trembling body and a shaking voice, I started telling my story. I didn't think anyone would care or want to hear it, but I would just tell it and get this over with.

As I was talking, the crowd grew quieter and quieter. I started telling them about my dad abandoning us and saying to my face that he didn't love me and had never wanted me. I think I told them that I was homeless when I was seventeen,

> *but I can't really remember because my mind blacked out. It was like the Holy Spirit took over and started talking through me. At one point, I asked people to come to the front stage area to get prayer, and I saw that everyone was crying and coming forward. Everyone. What a life-changing experience!*

Scan to see a clip of Lynzee's testimony.

It's a Dance-Off!

Trysten Pringle is a Home Church Bible College graduate who has been on many trips with me. He is so versatile. He can hug a sick child in the slums of Nairobi or take a last-minute opportunity to teach at a school of 700 students who heard there was a foreigner in town. He has even given his testimony in crowds of over 3,500 people.

How do we gather such a huge crowd? In general, Africans *love* music and dancing. So, we organize a dance competition and advertise it in the community. Hundreds show up. We offer a prize for the winner. The crowd grows larger. We start singing, then announce that we have a Canadian on the team (Trysten) who will challenge the winner of the dance competition. We call it a "Canada vs. DR Congo Dance-off."

Scan to see a clip from Trysten's trip.

This one day, the crowd grew to over 3,500 people. Of course, we used the opportunity to talk about the gospel of Jesus, share our testimonies, and invite people to attend the nearby Home

Church and begin their journey in Christianity. The majority of the people lifted their hands to accept Jesus after Trysten shared the Bible and his testimony. It was so exciting! Then we had the finale of the street event. We presented the prize to the local dance-off champion, then we did a dance-off with Trysten and the new DR Congo champ. Trysten performed his joyous dance moves that included "the worm" and back-flips. The crowd cheered and shouted.

We stayed in the area for a couple of days, visited many people living in the refugee camps, and fed over 700 children.

> **TRYSTEN:** *One of the greatest memories for me was in DR Congo when we were conducting a feeding program at our new Home Church near a refugee camp in Minova, DR Congo.*
>
> *I noticed a small child who seemed to be waiting patiently for his food. Seven hundred hungry kids are not patient when they see the food arrive. I took him aside so we could talk as he ate his plate full of rice, potatoes, and a few pieces of meat. I asked him when he had last had a meal like this, and he said that he had never had a meal like that before in his life! I cried. I was so thankful to be able to give him the best meal that he'd ever had. I prayed for him and his family right there. That story rocked me. This is why I continue to sponsor Home of Hope.*

Part of the crowd gathered for the dance-off.

Josh Hill was another member of our team in DR Congo. He later told me, "My trip with Home of Hope was the highlight of my life and was so fulfilling! There is so much more value going on a trip like this than going on an all-inclusive vacation holiday."

When Josh and I saw the hundreds of kids in the Buganga refugee camp in North DR Congo, we prayed together for direction

from God for how we could help these kids and this needy area. We received it! We asked our Home Church area pastor to meet with the refugee camp chief and ask if he would give us land if we would promise to help hundreds of children. The chief gave us land to build our church and a training center. We gave 100 tarps to cover the straw huts and 300 health cards. We now feed about 400 hungry children every Saturday there through the feeding program.

Wisdom and negotiation can solve problems and create solutions. We are the only church in this camp and the only aid in the community. Now we are advancing in teaching about microloans and co-ops to help people make their own money.

The building we built in the Buganga refugee camp (pictured on the next page) is used for many things: church on Sunday, midweek training classes for many ages, weekly feeding programs, and a training center for microloans and co-ops to help women with their futures. Recently there was a lot of rain, the whole camp flooded, and the straw huts filled with water. Many people moved inside the church to stay dry.

Ministry Trips vs. Discovery Tours

While some people want to go on a trip to visit and serve rescued children, Josh wanted to go on a teaching trip. He, as a businessman, wanted to teach the Bible. I said, "Okay, let's go!"

He commented quite a few times about how eager the people

were to listen and learn from him. He noticed how they would soak up every word he said and how easy it was to share with such amazing people. He wants to go back very soon.

Other people who go on teams prefer not to stand on a stage and speak, but would rather help with the many HOH projects. We call these trips Discovery Tours. Anyone can apply to join a Discovery Tour to help children and the poor in various countries.

Those who sponsor children can also apply to meet their sponsored child face to face. People often find this to be an incredibly emotional experience! There is a family connection between many sponsors and their sponsored children that goes far beyond providing basic physical needs. It is awesome when fathers come on a tour with me to "visit the fatherless" and when mothers come to cuddle the babies.

I love playing the guitar and singing songs to the children at the Kenya Dream Centre as they get ready for bed. I did this often with our children when they were little. One of my favorite songs is *Jesus Loves Me, This I Know*. It is so powerful to hear these sweet little voices sing *Jesus loves me*. It brings tears to my eyes to see them understand more about Jesus and realize that only Jesus can give them the full healing they need. These children are not just being cared for physically but spiritually as well. We point them to Jesus and hope that they establish their own faith in Him.

The picture on the next page sums up this chapter so well. It is priceless to see five rescued children in Nairobi and how they have grown over the years! It is a powerful reminder of why we are doing what we are doing and who we are doing it for.

I am so thankful that God transformed my heart from being the person who used to change the channel when I saw stories of children in need. And I am grateful for all those who have joined me on trips, or even led trips of their own, to love and serve these children.

13. GOATS ON MOTORCYCLES

I MENTIONED EARLIER THAT THE BEST WAY TO HELP CHILDREN is to help their mothers. We strongly believe that children thrive best in their own families. Therefore, giving mothers business opportunities and training that empowers them to provide for their household is one of the greatest things we can do for families.

While our feeding programs and child sponsorships continue to save lives and provide for immediate needs, we are particularly excited about the potential that our animal projects, school projects, and other programs have to affect thousands of people over the long term. These initiatives are helping to break the cycle of poverty and build a sustainable future for countless people. I'd like to share stories from some of these projects that illustrate the life-changing power of investing in people's futures.

One of the most effective ways to help families is to provide animals they can use to produce income. We call this form of assistance "animal projects." The story below, told by my good friend Melanie, makes a great introduction to the idea.

I somehow managed to talk Melanie into *carrying a goat on a motorcycle* to a mother living in a mud hut in Rwanda. Melanie is a reserved, professional woman, and to see her holding a goat while riding a motorbike was priceless. The way she tells the story makes me laugh so hard.

MELANIE: *The time had come to deliver the goats and pigs so generously purchased by my friends and family. There were four motorcycles; four drivers (three hired drivers who didn't speak English, plus my son Garrick); and four cargo holders, including Karissa, an interpreter, our bookkeeper, me, and a guide who also didn't speak English, plus a bunch of squealing pigs and bawling goats!*

When they brought me the biggest goat, I thought they were crazy. I outright refused: no! When they brought me a smaller, wailing goat, I wondered, do goats bite? When they gave me the goat with its feet tied together, I wondered, who is stronger, me or the goat?

When we started driving, I wondered if I would go flying off the back of the motorcycle since both of my hands were actively engaged in holding the goat, and there was no backrest on the bike. When we pulled onto the highway, I wondered if we would be hit by a bus in the crazy Rwanda traffic. Then, when the goat's back feet came untied, I wondered if I was strong enough to hold on to her. As we drove along the edge of a steep hill, I closed my eyes so I couldn't see. I'm afraid of heights, and I knew I might panic and shift my weight the wrong way, sending the bike off balance.

In between all of these wonderings and ponderings, the view of the countryside was riveting and captured my attention. That is, until yet another set of thistles going through my jeans jerked me back to the reality that I was on the back of a motorcycle driven by a stranger who didn't speak English, going up a winding dirt road, carrying a bawling goat whose feet had now come untied. It just doesn't get any better.

When we made our first stop, they told me the bikes

couldn't go the rest of the way, so I had to carry the goat up the hill. Halfway up, the goat freaked out, took hold of my hair with its mouth, and wouldn't let go! A goat was eating my hair, and there was nothing I could do about it.

After we got to the top of the incline, we came to the home of a woman named Jacqueline, who was standing outside with her three small children, waiting for us. I was grateful to receive help getting the goat unattached from my hair and giving my sore arms a much-needed break.

Jacqueline invited us into her home. The main room was about a five-by-eight-foot space with a dirt floor. There wasn't a single piece of furniture: not a blanket or a pot or a mat. However, she was proudly and generously welcoming me into all that she had.

With the help of the interpreter, I found out her name and the names of her children. I prayed for her and told her I hoped the goat would be a great help to her family. At the end, she hugged me, thanked me, and began to sob. She hung on and continued crying. I might have just given her the greatest hope for her future she had ever received, yet it seemed so small compared to the magnitude of her need. I felt like I was being inhumane. I have so much.

I was very impacted by her deep gratitude for what we had done for her. The fear I had felt when I was handed the goat quickly faded from my mind, replaced by the knowledge that I was delivering a lifeline to a desperate family.

Lives were changed that day. The question is, who was changed more: them or me? It was the best day of my entire trip.

We received an update on that family seven years later. The same goat is alive and doing well, and it is reproducing and helping this family to this day. What a wonderful gift!

The family is very involved in serving at the local feeding program. The mother, Jacqueline, says, "Thanks to God for His mercy and provision!"

Animal Projects

Melanie's goat is just one of many animals we have been able to provide for families in need. I learned the power of raising animals many years ago, growing up on a farm in Canada. When I was around twelve years old, my dad told me that he would give me a baby pig of my own if I worked hard every day for a month. I had to clean out the pig pens and feed the pigs before and after school. It was hard work!

At the end of the month, I chose my favorite black-and-white female piglet to raise. Four months later, she was old enough to get pregnant; four months after that, she had eight baby pigs. I faithfully fed the piglets and cleaned out their pens. We sold the male pigs when they were about three or four months old, and I made $200 on each pig!

I had made about $1,000. Wow, did that feel good! I still remember how excited and free I felt. I no longer needed to beg my dad for money to buy a chocolate bar or anything else because I could buy it myself.

I kept the female pigs to continue to have babies. These pigs became my best friends. That might sound funny, but it was true!

The opportunity and training my father gave me were invaluable. I have been able to pass along what I have learned to help others in many nations become self-sufficient. Wherever we serve people, we do our best to empower them to earn their own money.

For example, every teen in rural Rwanda who receives monthly sponsorship gets their own pig or goat. Many teens choose a goat because they are not as dirty as pigs, and they eat almost anything. We have also given rabbits, chickens, cows, and other animals. These animals belong to the teens, and they are responsible for caring for them. The teens learn how to work, make and manage money, and build a business.

When I went to Malawi to help start churches and lay a foundation for HOH there, the country was in a time of severe famine. Malawi is often said to be the third poorest country in the world. Despite their economic disadvantage, the people I have met in Malawi are loving, peaceful, and hardworking. A large percentage of the population are farmers, and farming is very close to my heart.

We introduced the animal project to our Malawi team and told them what we were doing in other countries. In the first village we visited, the local village chief attended our outdoor meeting, and I gave her a proposal. "If you can give us a place where ten women can care for ten goats, I have a sponsor who will buy the goats."

She was excited, and she walked me over to a parcel of land and said, "I will give this land for the project."

We started our first animal co-op there. Our HOH leader, Simon, is doing an outstanding job. He met with the village chief and the local pastor, and they chose the ten women. Simon supervised the project and helped them build a little pen, then he bought and delivered the goats. He sent us pictures, and he shared photos and stories on social media as well. Many other people got involved by donating to this project. Home of Hope now has animal co-ops in many of our fourteen projects in Malawi, and we will soon be entering Mozambique. To date, we have helped more than 100 single mothers and their families by providing goats.

Each member of the co-op shares the duties of feeding, car-

ing for, and protecting the goats. All the women are so excited to get their own goat in the herd. It is a little light at the end of a long tunnel of poverty.

Animal projects are a great complement to preaching the gospel in new areas. Our Home Church overseer, Pastor Jonathan Banda, is a wonderful man who loves praying, teaching, preaching, and sharing Jesus in remote areas where very few plant churches. He has great compassion for the poor and orphans, and he also has a deep burden to help older adults. Many older people have no one caring for them. We are expanding Home of Hope's vision to help more of the elderly and widows. Jonathan's heart reminds me of 1 Timothy 5:3, "Take care of widows who are destitute.... This pleases God immensely" (MSG).

The animal projects in India are exciting as well. They are growing, which is helping to produce supplemental income for our boarding school. Andrew even has an arrangement with local restaurants that buy our purebred goat meat! They also have many cows that provide income from the sale of milk and meat. Selling the dung for fertilizer is another source of income.

Currently, the government of India is disallowing all foreign funding to care for orphans. So we are teaching our leaders how to become self-sustaining as quickly as possible. Animal projects are so important and work exceptionally well. The Home of Hope team also raises several crops, including peanuts, rice, and vegetables.

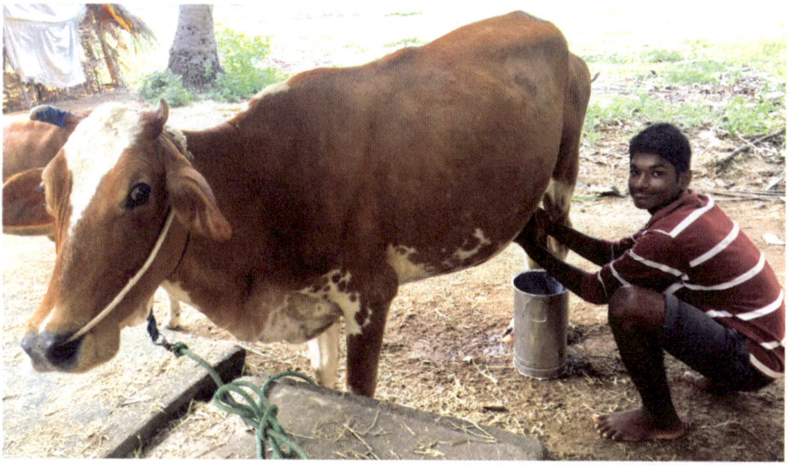

Medical Projects

Our medical projects help children and families in various ways. I mentioned earlier how important health cards are. It is exciting that the governments of DR Congo and Rwanda have implemented programs to help make health care affordable. For only $6 (CAD), a child can obtain a health card that will allow them to receive free medicine for 12 months. Six dollars for an entire year? That is about the cost of a specialty coffee! We have been able to purchase many health cards through the generosity of our sponsors.

In addition, if we find children who are suffering from extreme malnutrition, we provide a daily porridge filled with nutrients for six months. This is the recommended course of action from health professionals, and with time, it reverses the effects of malnutrition. After that, the children generally receive help through our weekly feeding programs, and we work with the mothers to receive training and opportunities through microloans.

Another way we have served in the area of health is through malaria prevention. Malaria is a terrible killer in the world, but it is preventable with mosquito nets. Many of our teams have raised

Children excited to receive their new health cards.

money to purchase family-sized mosquito nets and then installed them in people's huts. Malaria is treatable with medication, which is included with the health cards.

We have been blessed by the many medical professionals who have traveled on teams to help with our Home of Hope projects. For example, Dr. Johann van der Vyver came on a trip with me, and he was incredible. He worked extremely hard and attended to hundreds of children every day.

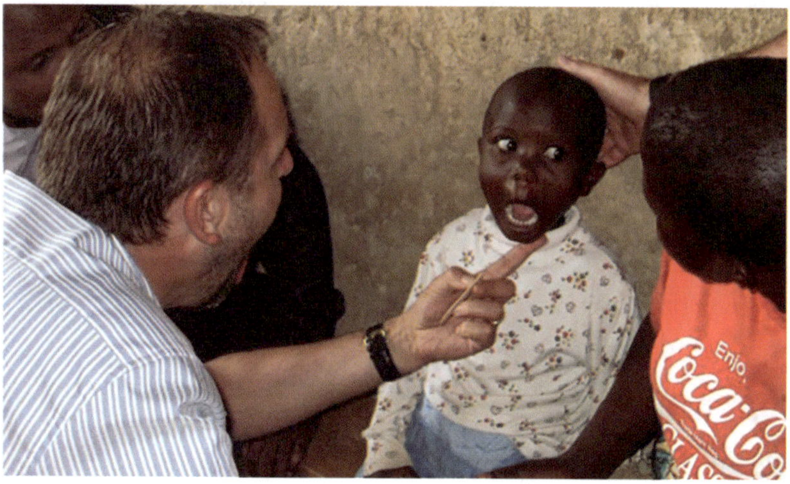

Our plan each day was to leave the hotel after breakfast at eight o'clock, but Dr. Johann said, "There are so many children in the village who need medical attention. I want to go out earlier. Who wants to come with me in the first van going to the area?" He loves people so much that we would almost have to drag him away at the end of the day as we had to leave before dark.

> **DR. JOHANN:** *My introduction to Home of Hope was around 2008, and soon after that, I went on my first trip to Rwanda. I recall the experience as if it was yesterday. It was truly the most exciting and greatest experience of my life as*

a physician and as a believer.

The first years in medicine for me were about learning and practicing some skills, but since connecting with Home of Hope and seeing the work firsthand, I began living in the understanding of what serving and helping people is all about. Patients are not just patients anymore, but they are people I can touch, talk to, and love.

It is impossible to go to Rwanda and Kenya and leave unaffected and unchanged. It forces one to look with new eyes on people in need, to pray for those in poverty, and to give more to those who have little. Being part of Pastor Brian's passion and vision is a privilege for me.

Dr. Johann inspecting the quality of food at the feeding program.

I love seeing the lives of people changed on ministry trips. Just as my heart was changed the first time I visited Rwanda, God used this trip to enlarge Dr. Johann's heart.

Life is about so much more than having a job and making money. When we reach out, we find that helping people is very fulfilling and a big part of God's plan for us.

School Projects

Another one of the ways HOH helps children is to make sure they receive an education. Providing desperate children with food to stay alive is vital, but it is also essential that they attend school so they can have a better future. Every child is **Meant 4 More**, but children with no education have little chance of rising out of poverty.

We have started schools in many countries where there is a need as well. Sometimes there are no schools for many miles. Some of our schools are for kindergarten children so that they don't have to walk all those miles to a public school until they are a bit older. This "WE NEED SCHOOL" picture helped us raise money for our first school in Rwanda. We are thankful for so many sponsors who have helped build and start schools and who cover tuition costs.

In Kenya, Beatrice Tsindori is an outstanding teacher who has taught the rescued children ever since the Dream Centre began over nine years ago. She started teaching them with storybooks

and homeschool-style lessons. Some of the children were rescued as toddlers, so a playschool and kindergarten became necessary.

When Beatrice began teaching, she was volunteering her time. Eventually, a few sponsors started supporting her as the teacher. In 2017, Beatrice started an official school. The school has grown, and there are now twenty-five rescued Dream Centre children attending. Ten children attend from a nearby children's home, and the rest are community children who pay a small tuition to attend.

There are 66 students from age three up through grade two. As the Dream Centre children get older, she will add another year to the school. Her goal is to have 150 students.

Not only is Beatrice leading our Dream Centre school, but she and her husband Samuel have taken in six of the rescued Dream Centre children into their home (see picture on the following page). This is one of our Family Units for a long-term home for rescued kids. They are an amazing couple!

We have several schools in rural villages like Cyuru, Rwanda, where people can sponsor a child's school tuition for as little as $5 (CAD) a month. Education is so vital for each of these children to become successful and break the poverty cycle. Donations are gladly accepted as there is a tremendous need for more schools in order to give these children a promising future.

Shoe Projects

During our weekly feeding projects, we noticed that many of the children had no shoes. Sometimes, we would see children with sores on their feet. Some children have never had a pair of shoes in their lives.

Our Rwandan project manager is Aime Habimana. He describes how he began the shoe project in Rwanda.

> **AIME:** *I have lived in Kigali, the capital of Rwanda, for several years. I have worked in non-profit organizations, business, finance, hospitality, and administration. When I started working with Home of Hope, my eyes were opened to the poverty in the rural villages. One day, on Home of Hope business, I was in a small rural village named Kigaga, and I noticed that very few children were wearing shoes or sandals. It disturbed me to realize that children in the city have many pairs of shoes, but here in this village, kids don't even own a single pair.*

I started to ask questions, and I was told that the few children with shoes were wearing adult-sized hand-me-downs from their grandparents or relatives. The majority of the children in that area had never received a new pair of shoes. I noticed that some siblings were actually sharing one pair and taking turns wearing them each day.

To me, this was terrible, and I had to do something about it. It captured my heart, and I made a new goal that year to get as many children a pair of shoes as I could.

I shared this goal and passion with Pastor Brian. He gave me advice on how to express my desire to the donors. I created a post on social media and received so much positive feedback. People started donating to the cause! I was so excited that I was able to be the solution to this simple problem for these kids!

We all know that shoes protect our feet from injuries and the elements, but we often overlook the fact that they also protect us from diseases and infections. Shoes are a lifeline.

My wish is to expand this project in many countries where Home of Hope is operating, but my passion for this project does not end there. I dream about starting a factory to create shoes so that we can provide children with shoes for a fraction of the cost—and help more kids! In addition to that, we would be creating jobs for some teenagers in our locations to work in the factory.

Of course, our ultimate goal is to lead people to Jesus, and what better way than by giving them something they need for free and telling them that salvation in Jesus is also free.

I am grateful to Pastor Brian for believing in me and allowing me to have a vision and see it fulfilled!

I am so glad we have a team of people who love what they are doing! Many people, like Aime, see a need and take the initiative to come up with an action plan to find a solution. Others, like Simon or Beatrice, have sacrificed to help children without any promise of a salary. They are all advancing in their calling and destiny.

I remember what the apostle Paul said about Timothy: there was no one like him, who naturally cared for people. So many people tend to be selfish and just care about themselves and how things will benefit them. He wrote, “I have no one else like him, who will show genuine concern for your welfare. For everyone looks out for their own interests, not those of Jesus Christ. But you know that Timothy has proved himself, because as a son with his father he has served with me in the work of the gospel” (Philippians 2:20-22 NIV).

Home of Hope is so blessed to have a dream team in every nation where we work. There is no way we could ever do what we do without such quality people. Thank you, team!

14. FOREVER CHANGED

Dan Peters often talks about his travels, and he connects many people to Home of Hope everywhere he goes. After one of his trips, he was telling stories in his local church. A friend of his, Dan Wiebe, was very moved by the story about Vishwa, the abandoned boy in India whom I wrote about earlier. Dan Wiebe has been connected with Home of Hope ever since. Since that time, he has been on three trips with HOH and is fulfilling his dream of making a difference in people's lives. He even took his two sons with him to see the Home of Hope projects. Here is his story.

> **DAN:** *I was touched by the boy's pain of not feeling wanted by his family. To think that a parent could call their child ugly was hard to believe. My heart was stirred, and I wanted to use the way God was blessing me in business to help others. I was understanding more and more how I was in business for a higher purpose. I wanted to use my business to make a dif-*

ference in people's lives.

I love sponsoring many things Home of Hope does, from the programs that feed thousands of children every week to rescuing children from many terrible situations. My wife and I have an ongoing desire to help just one more. I love visiting the Kenya Dream Centre and, as a father, loving on children who don't have a loving father.

It was astonishing to see how much I received when I started helping others. The Bible says it is more blessed to give than to receive, and I was starting to really experience this first-hand. I am reaping so much more than I have ever given. God multiplies what we do back into our own hearts.

Proverbs 11:24 says, "The world of the generous gets larger and larger; the world of the stingy gets smaller and smaller" (MSG).

It is not about my life; it is about fulfilling what God has called us to do. Pastor Brian and Home of Hope have given me an avenue to fulfill my purpose. God's plan is always to use us to make a difference in this world.

I feel so much love for these rescued children. God is love. We are called to love others. Loving those less fortunate is truly doing the will of God.

One of the other ways I feel I can help as a businessman is to offer vocational training, especially to some of the Home of Hope sponsored children who are now teens. I heard many teens were hoping to go to university someday, which is good, but the percentage of graduates who find jobs is quite low.

I wanted them to understand that with a strong work ethic and a positive outlook on life, they can be successful. I shared my testimony that I didn't even finish school but got busy in the trades. I encouraged young adults to look into possible trades where they could make a living, like fixing automobiles or motorcycles and working on a variety of building projects, to name a few.

One of the young people I taught is Jean Marie, whose story is told below. I have had the joy of watching him take to heart my words of training. He has grown so much, and I am proud of him!

Entrepreneurs in the Making

Here is the story of Jean Marie, the young man Dan Wiebe mentioned above, told in his own words.

JEAN MARIE: *Hello friends, my name is Jean Marie Nizeyimana, and I am twenty-five years old. I would like to share my testimony with you about where God took me and how He has treated me so well.*

I became an orphan when I was only two years old. I lived with my grandmother, who told me my parents had died. She was very poor, and, at the age of 80, she couldn't work anymore. When I was in primary school, after school I would carry water and look for firewood to cook some food. I would also go to the neighbors and ask if they could give us some

food or some coins. It was a very difficult time. It was hard to get food, clothes, and school materials. After my grandmother died, I was left alone.

At this time, Home of Hope, led by Pastor Brian, arrived in our village in Jabana, Rwanda. I was accepted by Home of Hope and immediately transferred with seven other orphans into a family unit with a nice caregiver taking care of all eight of us. With the help of a monthly sponsor and this home, I was able to go to church and eventually became the worship leader, a ministry I'm still involved in today. I also finished my secondary schooling and received a diploma in building construction.

On one of the Home of Hope teams from Canada, I met Dan Wiebe in one of our vocational training classes. He taught us how to get more training and change our thinking to become successful. He gave us many ideas on how we could make money with bricks.

I was very interested, and he taught a few of us how to make bricks with the brick machine that had been donated. I began making bricks very quickly. Then the Rwafandi Home Church needed a building. I not only learned how to make the bricks needed for the building, but I supervised the building project. This project helped me and many others to have employment. Many other sponsored teenagers learned

a trade as well to help them and their futures. Thanks very much, Dan, because you helped me learn how to make money.

Recently, we had a youth conference where young people from many Home Churches all over Rwanda came together, and I met a beautiful girl named Fiellete. She was also an orphan and lived in a Home of Hope family unit in her village of Cyuru. We fell in love. With my training in building and money saved from sponsorship and my brick-making business, I am now married and live in a house that I built. We had a wonderful wedding in December 2020. I am so thankful to God, to Home of Hope, and to my sponsors who have helped me so much! I am thankful for the good life I have.

We have also started a brick-making business in India, made possible by a sponsor who provided funds for a microloan. This business is an excellent way to teach older orphan boys how to work hard and make money for themselves. They are learning to save money for their college or university tuition. They are also using the bricks to construct five new buildings for the new school. There are no other brick-making businesses nearby, so they can fill orders for thousands of bricks for new customers.

Rescuing Street Kids in Bukavu, DR Congo

Pastor Ephrem Cirego and his wife, Deborah, are Home Church pastors in Bukavu, DR Congo, who are reaching out to teenagers living on the streets. Over 100 have been found so far, sleeping in back alleys, old junky cars, and abandoned buildings. They sometimes wrap their legs in plastic bags for warmth and protection from bugs. Ephrem and Deborah had compassion on them and gathered together some money from their church to start giving them occasional meals and lots of love.

Then they had an idea. There was no place to buy crushed gravel in the city, so they started a business with the older teens.

Clear goggles, mauls and hammers, and a truckload of big rocks were donated. The older teens take turns hammering the big rocks into crushed gravel that they can sell for a profit. There is now enough money to buy some food each day to help these street teens. Plus, they are being taught valuable life lessons like saving money to buy necessities and to eventually find a better place to sleep.

Pastor Ephrem and our Home of Hope team came up with a plan

for the younger teens to sell charcoal door to door like we are doing with many micro-loan co-ops with the women. The young teens are not working for anyone but themselves. Ten of them were given an initial

pail of charcoal, and they sold the charcoal door-to-door. Most of the community needs charcoal every day to burn for cooking food. These young teens are starting to make $3 to $5 USD a day for themselves. They take some of the profit they make and buy food.

This program makes it possible to give them a hand up, not a handout. It is such great training and instruction in valuable life skills. They are working with their hands and earning money every day, rather than turning to crime and violence. The project is growing, and we are now looking for better, safer places for them to sleep. Following that, we want to find ways to get these teens into school.

Pastor Ephrem teaching the boys about Jesus and training them for their futures.

Erick is a teen whose life has been influenced by pastors Ephrem and Deborah. Erick's parents were killed by some neighbors over a disagreement. He stayed with his grandmother until she also died.

He was left to wander the streets, begging for food and looking for somewhere to sleep. He is now part of the rescue mission. Someone heard his story and bought him some new clothes and shoes. He will be going to school when the next semester starts.

A woman in the Bukavu Home Church has invited him to stay in her house because he can make money selling charcoal to pay for his own food. She was given a microloan to help make some money for herself as well.

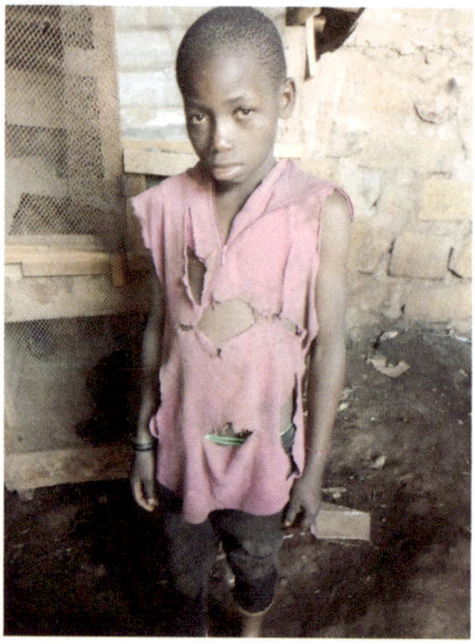

We are always looking for ways to help other children like Erick, serving communities by finding new ways to solve issues. Our HOH action plan is to identify needs and then develop the most effective, self-sustaining strategies possible to serve people in need.

Microloans Are Changing Lives in Nairobi

> **JANET:** *Jane was a desperate woman who had been rejected by her parents. When we first met her, she had tried several times to end her own life. She started spending nights*

in bars and selling herself to men so she could get food.

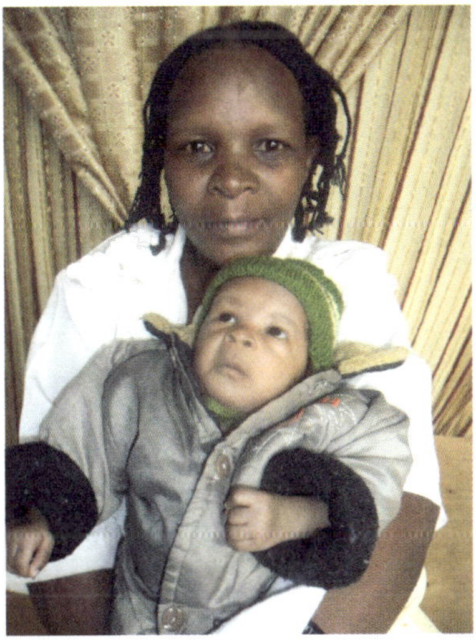

When she found herself pregnant, her first thought was abortion because she already had two sons who were ten and thirteen. She felt it was shameful to now be pregnant, and even more shameful to have a child whose father was unknown.

Jane agreed to meet with us, and we loved and counseled her for months. She accepted Jesus and decided to keep the baby after birth. One of the names she gave the baby boy was Brian, after Pastor Brian, whom she encountered in one of the training times that changed her life.

Jane was accepted into our business training school to learn about microloans to start a business. She now has a successful business that has allowed her to become self-sustaining.

Jane, proudly showing the store she owns.

Elroy's Legacy Continues

It was such a privilege to have Elroy's son, Mark Pankratz, travel with me to Africa. He wanted to see first-hand all that his dad spoke about for so many years and to help continue his legacy.

> **MARK:** *I will never forget the Sunday morning before my dad, Elroy Pankratz, left for Africa. He had been there before, but this time was different. My dad and mom, Nancy, were moving to Rwanda for a few months to help establish a new ministry called Home of Hope with our long-time friend and ministry partner Brian Thomson.*
>
> *As we gathered to pray that morning, there was a fire burning in my dad's heart. He had fallen in love with the people of Africa. Dad was seventy years old and had retired from active ministry. Most men his age would be golfing or fishing, but not my dad. He was about to embark on a new adventure. He was meant for more! As we prayed for my dad, I felt the Lord speak to me that in the next ten years, my parents would touch more lives than they had in all their previous years of ministry combined.*
>
> *The ministry grew tremendously over the next few years as local leaders were established and trained. Dad would come home and weep as he spoke of the people of Rwanda. From there, Dad went to the slums in Nairobi and witnessed some of the most desperate people in the world struggling to survive.*
>
> *For twelve years, we supported my dad as he traveled back and forth to Africa with Pastor Brian. Churches multiplied, and orphans, widows and young men were helped in significant ways. Over the years, we helped five of our children go on trips to Africa with my dad and Pastor Brian, but I*

had never made the trip. I believe one of the best things you can do for the next generation is get them out of their world and their comfort zone and give them a vision of something more.

Whenever we would talk about the ministry in Africa, my dad would weep, not just because of the physical needs and suffering he saw, but because of people's eternal value to Jesus. He longed for them to know Jesus more than anything, as he believed that is where lasting transformation would begin. I had planned to travel with my dad in the summer of 2019, but he had a stroke the year before, and he never made the trip to Africa again.

My first trip to Africa was with Pastor Brian and a businessman from our church named Andrew Tiel. As we traveled through Rwanda and Kenya, the people spoke of their love for my dad, Elroy. He was a real-life hero to them. His life had touched not just hundreds but multiplied thousands through the work of Home of Hope. When I asked why they loved him so much, they said, "because we knew how much he loved us!" I witnessed first-hand the results of the Home of Hope ministry: lasting change and transformation in the lives of people, one person at a time.

In Kariobangi, a slum in Nairobi, I met George Akelo. He was a dear friend of my dad and a key person who was working tirelessly to help the poorest of the poor. He took us on a tour through the slums. I have been to slums in other nations, but I had never seen the hopelessness and hardship I witnessed there. George's love for the people was very evident. He approached everyone, not just with kindness, but with a positive outlook and with hope. The Home Church in Kariobangi is a church on the weekend, but during the week it is a much-needed rescue center, of-

fering training to single moms which will help them succeed and establish small businesses so they can afford to move out of the slums. The land where Home Church is located is leased, and the lease is about to expire. Andrew and I knew that we needed to help this church.

Pastor Brian has a goal of fundraising to assist with the purchase of land so that Home Church has a permanent location. His vision is a possible second Dream Centre in Nairobi. It would be wonderful to see the Dream Centre vision expand beyond rescuing babies to include helping more widows, pregnant teen girls, and young men. It could enable this work that is already so effective in reaching

hundreds of people to possibly grow to impact thousands.

One of the things that surprised me was how simple it is to help. For just a small investment, you can help a whole family move from poverty in the slum to having their own business, which produces enough income to provide them with a living and afford schooling for their children. Their future and the generation to come is changed with a simple act of charity. It is a small gift with a huge impact.

Expansion of the Dream Centre Vision

Another person Elroy Pankratz inspired is Andrew Tiel. As a businessman, Andrew was deeply influenced by Elroy in their church in Penticton, B.C.

ANDREW: *Elroy helped me get closer to Jesus. He encouraged me to stop striving after empty things. And he encouraged me to go on a trip to Africa with Pastor Brian and Home of Hope.*

So, I went on a trip with Mark Pankratz (my pastor and Elroy's son) and Pastor Brian. After arriving in Nairobi, we went on a tour through one of the twenty-six slums in the city. It was so disturbing to see things such as a mother and her four children living in a shack less than ten feet square, about the size of many Canadian bathrooms. And they would be cooking their little bit of food that day with charcoal, causing black smoke to fill their tiny homes, which of course is also terrible for their health.

I have worked hard and have been successful all my life. I had a goal to retire early. That was everything I wanted to do. I worked hard and tried big business, but eventually we lost millions of dollars, and I had to go back to work. This time, I am doing well. But I learned my lesson, and I am making different decisions. I am building my life on purpose and vision and pursuing the right things.

Mark and Andrew traveling to Nairobi.

Now, we are having so much fun in business. It makes life more enjoyable when you lock on to a purpose that is bigger than yourself. It is about God's purpose. It is not even just about His purpose for me, but about His BIG purpose.

Everything about business now is different for me. Even the stress of running a business feels different. Enjoying the accomplishments of business means so much more. So many people make money and spend all they earn, trying to fill the void in their lives. They get caught in this type of whirlwind routine. But when you are centered on Jesus and what He wants you to do, your life is full, and any-

Mark visiting the building his dad helped build in Jabana, Rwanda, with Emmanuel, the first sponsored child.

thing relating to business is on top of that. Now, my wife and I have decided to live on less and to give more. Enjoying the accomplishments means so much more because we are not just making money for ourselves alone; we want to reach out and help meet needs.

My trip to Africa changed my life. Now, every day, I think about the people I met there and new projects that I want to help with. I know God is blessing me in a greater way because He wants me to help more. I loved helping people who were so hungry to learn. They just needed the opportunity to be given the right tools and some basic training. Now, their lives are taking off! Each Home Church in Nairobi is not just a church; it is a rescue center. Much of what Home of Hope does in the world is a lifesaving ministry. Literally. When babies are being thrown away, we must do something. It is not just helping people—it is saving their lives.

Pastor Brian and the HOH team are praying about ways to enlarge the vision of the Dream Centre to help thousands more. Mark and I want to be part of the great work that HOH dreams of doing with expanded projects serving many people. We love what God is doing and want to help HOH with whatever they do in any country.

We are praying with Pastor Brian about how to expand the vision beyond the current Dream Centre that focuses on rescuing babies. One strong option is a second Dream Centre that would help rescue and empower teens, pregnant women, and mothers. We would also like to see liter-

> *acy classes created for those who want to learn to read, as well as classes that develop the business skills needed to launch self-sustaining projects. We are considering building a multi-level facility that includes leasable spaces for offices and stores to help provide revenue. This Dream Centre could help launch hundreds of microloans, co-ops, and food carts to assist thousands of women and over 10,000 children. I think it is also important to help the men. We met some men living in the slums. We provided them with three pigs, and these soon multiplied to seven pigs, then forty-two pigs. The men sold some of them and kept others so their herds could keep growing.*
>
> *I am committed to helping find solutions for the greatest needs I have ever seen in my life, and I encourage you to do the same.*

Part of our expanding Dream Centre vision is a commitment to being open 24/7 with many ministries focused on serving the needs of the poor and destitute. If you would like to find out more about the expansion of the Dream Centre vision, please go to www.homeofhope.ca or visit the Facebook page by scanning this QR code.

Growing Pains

The expansion of Home of Hope has been a process full of miracles, but that doesn't mean it has always been easy. We have had to face some disappointing situations as the ministry has unfolded.

In part, this is because God works with people. He uses humans like us, with our strengths and weaknesses, our hopes and fears, our wisdom and our foolishness. We don't always get it right. Sometimes course correction is required along the way.

In a few instances, we have had to deal with corruption, lying, selfishness, and unwise decisions among team members. When I read in the Bible about Paul being forsaken by Demas or harmed by Alexander the coppersmith, or about how Judas stole ministry money and then betrayed Jesus, I must admit that I can relate. However, we are committed to transparency and integrity in the work, both with our donors and those we serve. If and when things come to light, we address them head-on with courage and humility, knowing that even in our weaknesses, God is strong. Even though people might fail, God's plan never will. We have His promise that He uses all things for our good (Romans 8:28).

Building a legacy is never without a battle. Helping people is not always easy. But I will not give up! I am committed to seeking first the kingdom of God and His righteous lifestyle, to learning from mistakes, and to pressing on toward the high calling of God.

We strive both to be faithful ourselves and to train and empower faithful people. "Faithful" means to remain loyal and steadfast. Paul wrote, "The most important quality of one entrusted with such secrets is that they are faithful and trustworthy" (1 Corinthians 4:2 TPT). He told Timothy, "You have heard me teach things that have been confirmed by many reliable witnesses. Now teach these truths to other trustworthy people who will be able to pass them on to others" (2 Timothy 2:2 NLT).

This work is bigger than any one person, vision, or decision. It comes from God's heart, and we trust that He will lead us into the future with wisdom and courage.

15. YOU ARE MEANT 4 MORE

I LOVE THE TITLE OF THIS BOOK. God has such big plans for each of us, and we all have different callings, giftings, and purposes. You don't have to start a charity, feed children, or travel to other countries. That is my story and calling, but it might not be yours. I hope, however, that my stories and the dozens of stories I've shared in this book have inspired you to chase after the next chapter God has for you.

Do you know what your purpose is? Do you know what God's destiny and His calling for you are? Regardless of what God has done through you until now, there are always new things to discover about your purpose and calling. God always has more for you!

Jesus told the following parable about a man who went on a trip and gave his servants gold coins to administrate while he was gone. One of them multiplied his coin ten times over!

> *Luke 19:13, 16-17 (GNT)*
> Before he left, he called his ten servants and gave them each a gold coin and told them, "See what you can earn with this while I am gone."
>
> ...The first one came and said, "Sir, I have earned ten gold coins with the one you gave me."

> "Well done," he said; "you are a good servant! Since you were faithful in small matters, I will put you in charge of ten cities."

The point of this story is that much of our future depends on what we do now. Notice the enormous promotion this faithful servant received. He was set as a ruler over ten cities! The sad part of the story is that one servant did nothing with the resources he had been given. The master rebuked this servant and took the coin away from him.

We must do something with what God has given us. We cannot allow fear or anything else to hold us back from the future God has for us.

That brings us to the question, what does God have ahead for you? I can't answer that for you specifically, of course, but I can tell you I have seen many people discover another level of purpose *through helping others*. Miraculous things begin to happen when we use our resources to help others. God opens our hearts and minds. He gives us creativity, blessing, and finances. He pours out His compassion and love in us and through us.

Many times—every time—our greatest purpose comes from helping other people.

- Maybe, like Dan Peters, you are in business, and God has some adventures He would like to lead you on.
- Maybe, like Denis, you are great at fixing things or building things. You could have your life changed by going on a trip to help others in one of the poorest places on earth.
- Maybe, like Judah Ann, you know sign language, and you might find yourself equipped to show God's love to a deaf and mute boy who was tossed aside by his parents.

- Maybe, like JD and Joy, or like Shawn and John, you can sponsor a child who you will one day visit and meet in person. There is a great reward in visiting the fatherless! It is so close to the heart of God, and the feeling that floods your heart is unexplainable.
- Maybe, like me, you are middle-aged, and God has an entirely new direction for you. He has a purpose and a plan waiting for you. It could be a huge surprise!
- Maybe, like Elroy, you are in your golden years, and you can start doing something that you have dreamed about since you were young or that will have the most significant impact of your entire life.
- Maybe, like Melanie, you could deliver a goat to the poorest person you have ever met and give a mother hope that could change her life.
- Maybe, like Josh, you have always wondered what it would be like to stand in front of hundreds of people and tell your favorite Bible stories and feel the thrill as people listen to your teaching and learn from you.
- Maybe, like Janet, you had always planned to be an accountant, but instead, you find a life-changing vocation of rescuing women and teenage girls.

I am a practical guy, so I couldn't write this book without giving some real-life tips to unlock what's next for you. As I mentioned before, I seem to have the spiritual gift of pushing people into things they might not have done on their own. So if you'll allow me, I'd like to share with you a few things I've learned on my journey. These are principles I have seen play out time and time again in people from all over the world who have come to believe that they, too, are **Meant 4 More**.

God has led me on an amazing journey. I give Him all the glory because only He could have taken a simple farm boy who started off raising pigs (and preaching to them) and used him as a catalyst to bring hope and life to so many children and families in need.

I feel so grateful and fulfilled. But it didn't just happen by chance. Many things contributed to both discovering and walking in the will of God. I pray that these tips, suggestions, and principles will help you understand His plan for your life.

1. Get Closer to Jesus

I am not talking about religion or some external set of rules that you must conform to. Christianity is all about having a personal relationship with Jesus, and I encourage you to pursue a relationship with Him in every possible way.

Connie and I have been married since 1979. We both chose to give our lives to Jesus when we were sixteen years old. We are both dedicated and committed to doing whatever Jesus wants us to do (John 2:5). We have read the Bible together all these years. Even when I am traveling, we follow the same Bible reading plan. We pray together, and we keep Jesus as the center of our lives.

One of my favorite verses is John 14:6, where Jesus says, "I am the [only] Way [to God] and the [real] Truth and the [real] Life; no one comes to the Father but through Me" (AMP). Jesus is the *only* way, the *only* truth, and the *only* life; there is no other way to heaven than through Jesus!

Jesus poured *His love* into my heart (Romans 5:5), and that made all the difference. I was self-focused, thinking primarily about myself and what I wanted to do. Jesus is the one who changed my heart.

You can't draw close to Jesus without being changed by His love, and when you are changed, you'll find yourself growing in love toward others. His presence makes all the difference because He pours out His love in your heart.

> **PUT IT INTO PRACTICE:** *The closer we get to Jesus, the more we will understand His plans for our lives. Draw near to Jesus every day, and He will draw near to you (James 4:8). If you have never asked Jesus into your life, I invite you to do so now. I had believed in God all my life, but it was not until I was sixteen years old that my eyes were opened, and I asked Him to forgive me. With a simple prayer, Jesus came into my life.*
>
> *Romans 10:9, 10 (NLT)*
> *If you openly declare that Jesus is Lord and believe in your heart that God raised him from the dead, you will be saved. For it is by believing in your heart that you are made right with God, and it is by openly declaring your faith that you are saved.*

2. Pursue God's Specific Assignment for You

As you pray, ask the Lord to reveal more of His plan for you. The great apostle Paul found his purpose, and he spoke these words, which have become an anchor for me.

> *Acts 20:24 (NLT)*
> "But my life is worth nothing to me unless I use it for finishing the work assigned me by the Lord Jesus—the work of telling others the Good News about the wonderful grace of God."

We are all on this planet for a reason. There are too many people missing their callings and wandering through life empty and unfulfilled—Christians included! God wants to fill our lives with adventure, fulfillment, and purpose so that we can look forward to every day.

> *Philippians 3:14 (KJV)*
> I press toward the mark for the prize of the high calling of God in Christ Jesus.

> **PUT IT INTO PRACTICE:** *Read the amazing Bible verse below several times while you talk to God about it. Allow it to give you fresh faith in your heart for your future. God has something so remarkable for each of us, something that has never come into our minds before.*
>
> *1 Corinthians 2:9 (NIV)*
> *As it is written: "What no eye has seen, what no ear has heard, and what no human mind has conceived—the things God has prepared for those who love him."*

3. Read the Bible Daily and Expect God to Speak to You

Reading the Bible is one of the most important ways God can speak to us. Often, when I pray about a decision, the next time I read the Bible, there is a verse with the exact answer to what I am asking God about. In particular, reading Proverbs is practical and helpful. Connie and I have read a chapter of Proverbs almost every day for most of our years of marriage. There is so much real-life wisdom for everyday happenings and challenges.

We can never fulfill God's total will for our lives without the Bible. I will never forget what a Bible college teacher taught me as a young man. He said, "God's word is His will, and God's will is His word! If you ever want to know God's will, read His word. His word reveals His will."

The Holy Spirit wants to guide your next steps, and He will often use the Bible to reveal what those steps are. So, as you read the Bible, note any key verses that stand out to you.

Some people explain it this way: "As I was reading the Bible, a verse jumped off the page." When this happens, I encourage you to stop immediately and spend more time reading it over and over. With online tools, it is easy to study the key words in verses that come alive to you in more detail. It is vital to meditate on those portions of scripture. Think about them over and over as you go about your day. It is not just reading the Bible but meditating on it that promises us a successful future.

> *Joshua 1:7 (NLT)*
> Study this Book of Instruction continually. Meditate on it day and night so you will be sure to obey everything written in it. Only then will you prosper and succeed in all you do.

Meditating on the word includes studying and learning about topics that are important to you. What is God's will about any subject that you want to know more about? Maybe you want to know more about healing, for example. Study God's Word and read many Bible verses on healing. Read for yourself what the Bible says. As you study *His Word*, you will begin to know for sure what *His will* is!

If you want to grow even more in your knowledge of the Bible, consider enrolling in Bible college classes. Going to Bible college was so good for me, and I would encourage every teenager or young adult (or adult of any age!) to attend Bible college so they can understand the Bible more and know Jesus better. You will become solid and strong in your Christian walk, which will help you in whatever vocation you are called to.

Whether you study the Bible formally or simply read it devotionally, day by day throughout your life—or both of those things!—the Bible will be a light for your path wherever you go. Just as you need headlights to drive a car in the dark, you need spiritual light to see where you are going in your life.

> *Psalm 119:105 (NLT)*
> Your word is a lamp to guide my feet and a light for my path.

Look at the Message translation of that verse. "By your words I can see where I'm going; they throw a beam of light on my dark path." I love that! By the way, one great way to study the Bible is to read verses in several translations. There are so many versions of the Bible that are free online.

The content of a verse is more important than the reference, but it's nice to be able to go back and find the passages that speak to you. Sometimes that takes a bit of creativity. One day, I was reading the Bible in my personal devotions, and I read Psalm 73:23,24.

> *Psalm 73:23, 24 (NLT)*
> Yet I still belong to you; you hold my right hand. You guide me with your counsel, leading me to a glorious destiny.

Wow, what a great verse, I thought, and I went on with my day. The next day, I remembered that verse as I was praying. I went looking for it, but I couldn't find it! I had read quite a few chapters in the Bible the day before, so I searched for that passage a long time before I finally found it. When I did, I repeated the reference a few times. *Psalm 73, verse 23*. It sounded easy to remember. The next day, I began thinking about that same verse. Yet again, I couldn't remember where it was.

At devotions with our family around the breakfast table, I told our kids, "I need your help. I can't remember this reference, even though I have tried and tried. It is Psalm 73:23 and 24. What can I do to remember it?"

Our son Ryan said, "Dad, haven't you heard the crazy Pizza 73 commercials on TV?"

I don't like commercials and skip over them as much as possible. So Ryan found the song online, and the jingle of the commercial started to go over and over in my mind. I don't sing Pizza 73, of course; I changed the lyrics in the commercial to say Psalm 73. To this day, I have never forgotten this particular scripture reference!

More importantly, though, I haven't forgotten the verse itself: "You guide me with your counsel, leading me to a glorious destiny." Isn't that amazing? God has a glorious destiny for each one of us! And He *wants* to take us by the hand, give us His counsel and wisdom, and lead us step by step into the calling He has for us.

> **PUT IT INTO PRACTICE:** *Read the Bible daily and get to know the God of the Bible more deeply. He is the sovereign God, the maker of heaven and earth. Your faith will increase as you read His word (Romans 10:17). Expect Him to speak to you from the Bible. As I read stories about heroes in the Bible like Moses or Abraham, I remind myself that God loves me just as much as He loved the people in the Bible. He had a plan for Daniel and Peter, and He has a plan for me. He doesn't have any favorites (Acts 10:34). You are important to Him, and He wants to reveal Himself to you.*

4. God Wants to Speak to You and Lead You in Your Prayer Life

Prayer is a key to understanding God's will for your life. As you pray, ask for His help.

God wants to lead each one of us. He wants to teach us to follow His Holy Spirit in our lives. He wants to be so close to us that He can guide us with just a look from His eye.

> *Psalm 32:8-9 (NKJV)*
> I will instruct you and teach you in the way you should go; I will guide you with My eye.
> Do not be like the horse or the mule, which have no understanding but must be controlled by bit and bridle or they will not come to you.

As we continually soften our hearts and stay hungry for God, He will speak to us and lead us. Some people say, "God never speaks to me." But the Bible says, "My sheep hear My voice, and I know them, and they follow Me" John 10:27 (NKJV) Spend time with God, be quiet and try to listen to Him speak to you.

> *Matthew 4:4 (The Message)*
> It takes more than bread to stay alive. It takes a steady stream of words from God's mouth.

As you've seen by now, I travel on a lot of airplanes. Once, just as I took my seat, the flight attendant announced, "Our airline is one of the few that allows you to listen in on the conversation between our pilot and the airport tower control."

I quickly followed the directions, put my headphones on, and listened to the many voices going back and forth so quickly with each other. All the pilots approaching the airport from many miles away were preparing to land, and they were talking with the tower and receiving instructions. There were other planes on the ground preparing to depart, and aircraft on various runways were lining up to take off. The pilots of those planes were also communicating with the tower.

It was all fascinating to me. They used words for the alphabet and numbers, such as *Echo* for the letter E, *Niner* for number nine, and so on. That way, each pilot would hear clearly and not miss any instructions. The voice in the tower would say, "Alpha, Bravo, Charlie, you are cleared for landing. Delta, Echo, Foxtrot, you are next for take-off." There were many pilots and many voices, but everything worked smoothly.

This is so much like the Christian life. We need to keep our spiritual headphones on and listen to the "tower," the Holy Spirit, all the time. The people in the tower see the larger picture. They know exactly where the pilot should fly and at what altitude, what the speed should be, and their exact coordinates.

Take a look at this picture. What is wrong with it? Maybe the pilot took off his or her headphones. Perhaps the pilot is arrogant and thinks, "I don't need the headphones. I don't need to listen to others. I can do this by myself! I have flown for so many years, so I know how it is done."

Only God knows the gifts He put inside of us. Only God knows His destiny for our lives. Keep your headphones on and listen for the special instructions from the Holy

Spirit every day. Spend time listening.

Anyone can learn to hear God's voice, even children. Just look at Samuel in the Bible.

> *1 Samuel 3:10 (NIV)*
> The LORD came and stood there, calling as at the other times, "Samuel! Samuel!" Then Samuel said, "Speak, for your servant is listening."

Long before Paul was a world-changing preacher and apostle, he was a ferocious persecutor of Christianity. If anyone was going the wrong way, it was Paul! He was known by the name Saul at the time, and the story of his 180-degree turn toward Jesus is found in Acts 9.

> *Acts 9:3-6 (NKJV)*
> As [Saul] journeyed he came near Damascus, and suddenly a light shone around him from heaven. Then he fell to the ground, and heard a voice saying to him, "Saul, Saul, why are you persecuting Me?"
>
> And he said, "Who are You, Lord?"
>
> Then the Lord said, "I am Jesus, whom you are persecuting. It *is* hard for you to kick against the goads."
>
> So he, trembling and astonished, said, "Lord, what do You want me to do?"

These eight words that the apostle Paul stated represent one of the greatest prayers we could offer to God every day. "Lord, what do You want me to do?"

Anyone can be led by what they *want*, or what they *feel*, or what they *think*. The most important thing, though, is to find out what God's will is. He knows best!

We need to make Jesus *Lord* of our lives, not just our Savior.

Asking Jesus to be our Savior is step one because faith in Him is the way to eternal life in heaven after we die. But step two is making Him our Lord now, on this earth. This is the key to going to the next level in this life.

> **PUT IT INTO PRACTICE:** *Sometimes I talk to God as the powerful Creator who created this wonderful planet and massive universe. Sometimes I talk to Him as my loving heavenly Father. "Our Father who is in Heaven..." (Matthew 6:9). Other times I talk to Jesus, who loved me and died on the cross for my sins.*
>
> *Do you have a set time to pray every day? If not, please consider starting devotions every day. If you don't know how, ask a Christian friend. They would love to help you.*
>
> *Pray a prayer like this every day and really mean it, and you will experience a breakthrough in your life. "Lord, what do You want me to do? I don't want it to be just about me anymore." Ask for His direction. Expect it. Then obey it.*
>
> *Galatians 5:25 (NLT)*
> *Since we are living by the Spirit, let us follow the Spirit's leading in every part of our lives.*
>
> *Let's keep our headphones on and listen to the Holy Spirit!*

5. Choose Your Friends Carefully

One of the keys to moving forward in your destiny is to choose friends who will not drag you down or influence you to go in the wrong direction. There are always people who will mock the things of God or laugh at you if you decide to follow God's will for your life. Some people will try their hardest to pressure you to go in the wrong direction or to become more like them. Psalm 1 is a powerful chapter that lays out how to be successful, stable, and fruitful.

> *Psalm 1:1-3 (NLT)*
> Oh, the joys of those who do not follow the advice of the wicked, or stand around with sinners, or join in with mockers. But they delight in the law of the LORD, meditating on it day and night. They are like trees planted along the riverbank, bearing fruit each season. Their leaves never wither, and they prosper in all they do.

You have probably heard that you will become like the people you hang out with. It is so true. Surround yourself with people who will push you toward your destiny.

> *Proverbs 13:20 (MSG)*
> Become wise by walking with the wise; hang out with fools and watch your life fall to pieces.

Elroy Pankratz is now in heaven, but he was the one who pushed me to go to Africa with him back in 1993. He had some connections in Kenya, so off we went to have crusades and teach pastors. Some of the people who received Jesus are now working with Home Church and HOH. One of them is a Home Church pastor in Nairobi who has six rescued children living with him. Another young man who attended those meetings oversees fourteen Home Churches in western Kenya and is starting to branch out into Uganda.

I mentioned before that Elroy insisted I go to DR Congo when I didn't want to. I thought I was too busy with things rapidly growing in Rwanda and Kenya. But now we have over forty Home Church locations in DR Congo, and we are helping thousands of children on remote islands, in refugee camps, and in villages, as well as street kids in big cities. Elroy became a great traveling companion to me, especially when everything started for Home of Hope in Rwanda in 2006—and he was seventy years old!

Many people want to retire because they think they have nothing else to contribute or just desire to relax for the rest of their lives. Elroy was full of passion and love. Many times, we would stay in hotel rooms together, and he would say in the middle of the night, "Brian, are you awake? Let's pray for tomorrow's projects."

He would start crying as he lay in bed praying at 2:00 a.m. for people to come to Jesus or asking God for strategies to help more children. I miss Elroy and his remarkable heart for people! He was a great friend who showed me how to love people better. Choose friends like Elroy!

> **PUT IT INTO PRACTICE:** *Evaluate your closest friendships. Which people are helping you in your life and pushing you to be better? Consider making a list of the friends you want to spend more time with, then sending a message to some of them right now.*

6. Journaling Makes Things Clearer

Often when I am seeking God about something or just praying about some concern, I will feel some impressions coming to me. Sometimes as soon as I begin writing or typing, a flow happens, and I will keep writing. Focusing on and writing things down is so important.

> *Habakkuk 2:2* (*GNT*)
> Write the vision. Make it clear on tablets so that anyone can read it quickly.

Maybe I pray a simple prayer, such as, "Jesus, if You were me in this situation, what would You do?" Or, "Jesus, if You walked into the room right now, what would You say to me?" So many times, I immediately start sensing impressions from the Lord, and I begin to write them down.

You can take special times of fasting and prayer and ask God what He has for your future and what His vision is for you. Then write down anything you are praying about and any dreams you have in your heart.

> *Proverbs 29:18 (KJV)*
> Where there is no vision, the people perish.

7. Pray For Dreams And Visions

The Bible refers to dreams often. There are many stories of dreams given for direction and guidance. Some dreams are meant to warn us or clarify God's leading for the future.

When I was seventeen years old and a new Christian, I was debating whether I should be a farmer or go to Bible college. One afternoon I was asking the Lord what I should do, and all of a sudden, I had a spiritual encounter. For a split second, I saw a giant yellow arrow pointing in the direction of the city where I was considering going to Bible college. It was like a vision. It was so real to me.

Classes had already started, though—about three weeks before. I wondered if I would be accepted or be able to attend. I went to my father and said, "Dad, I feel like God just told me that I should go to Bible college." For years he had told me that he wanted me to take over the family farm. I could tell he was disappointed, but he blessed me to go. I called the college, and they said they would allow me to start! Within an hour of the vision, I was in my car, driving to go to Bible college.

Today, over forty years later, I am in the ministry because of that clear, Spirit-led encounter.

> *Acts 2:17 (NLT)*
> "In the last days," God says, "I will pour out my Spirit upon all people. Your sons and daughters will prophesy. Your young men will see visions, and your old men will dream dreams."

Changes can happen quickly! Sometimes God gives us plenty of warning, and other times His direction can come in a moment. We need to be ready to move when He says go.

As I have gotten older, I often pray about the promise that older men will dream dreams. I see some older people who have retired pull back from serving God, wanting to rest and relax. That is okay. But God still wants to use us as we get older. Retired people often have *more* time to serve the Lord.

Many stories in the Bible show how God used older people. Moses was eighty when he started to lead Israel out of bondage. Caleb was eighty when he asked to be given a mountain in the Promised Land. The golden years are a prime time to stay active for the Lord and seek first His Kingdom to the very end.

Pray that God will "seal His instruction" with you as you sleep.

> *Job 33:15,16 (NKJV)*
> In a dream, in a vision of the night, when deep sleep falls upon men, while slumbering on their beds, then He opens the ears of men, and seals their instruction.

I love this verse, and it has become priceless to me. God has blessed me with many dreams. For years I kept a pen and paper by my bed, and now I keep a smartphone there. That way, it is easy to type out dreams in the middle of the night without turning on the light. If I don't write them down quickly, I forget them. I encourage you to cherish any time and any way that God speaks to you.

The most life-changing dream I've ever had was in Bible college. It had to do with dating, if you can believe it. Let me explain.

A few years earlier, before I was saved, I was looking forward to turning sixteen, getting my driver's license, and buying a car, because that meant I could ask a girl out on a date. I imagined going to the drive-in theatre and putting my arm around her. When I turned sixteen, though, our local drive-in theatre closed. That same year, I gave my life to Jesus. So, I didn't start dating until I was in Bible college.

I had seen other young men backslide when they began dating. I made a vow to God that I would stay faithful to Him and not follow their example. I prayed earnestly that God would make His will clear to me. In my dating and in every area of my life, I didn't want to waste my time or energy on bad decisions outside of God's will. I knew how important marriage was, and I longed for God's direction.

One night, God gave me a vivid dream. The dream was about me falling in love with a girl with blonde hair, a farm girl who had recently gotten saved and was in love with and on fire for Jesus. In my dream, she was giving her salvation testimony and talking about leading other young people to Jesus.

There was only one problem. The girl I had recently started to date had black hair. I really liked her, though, so I argued with the dream. I even asked a Bible college teacher and mentor in my life what I should do. He suggested I fast for seven days and pray, "Lord, not my will, but I want Your will for my life." He encouraged me to wait and listen during those seven days of fasting for God's will to become more evident.

I followed his suggestions. He was right: by the end of the fast,

I knew what I needed to do. The dream had gotten my attention, but spending time in prayer helped me see things from God's perspective. I realized we were not right for each other. I broke up with her, and I waited for God's choice before I would date again.

Not long after that, I found out that Connie, who I had known since I was in grade two, had given her life to Jesus. At the church's New Year's Eve party, she shared how she had recently given her life to Jesus and how exciting it was to receive the baptism of the Holy Spirit. She was bringing people to the youth group, and they were getting saved. And, of course, she was blonde! At that moment, I remembered my dream.

Over time, our friendship turned into romance. We have been married forty-two years and counting now, and we are still in love. She is—quite literally—the girl of my dreams!

God's will is good, acceptable, and perfect (Romans 12:1,2). Only God knew what woman could put up with me for so many years!

> **PUT IT INTO PRACTICE:** *Start a section in your notebook or phone where you can write down your dreams. Jot them down as soon as possible so that you don't forget them! Pray over dreams that you feel are from the Holy Spirit.*

8. Listen to Godly People and Ask For Counsel

I remember when I asked my pastor for some personal counsel. It was after I had been dating Connie for about six months. We were both serving Jesus and leading the youth group in one of our church locations in Alberta. I asked Pastor Mel for his advice. He asked me, "How long have you been dating?"

I answered, "six months."

"When do you think you will get married?"

"In two years."

He answered quickly, "She is a wonderful girl! Don't wait two years. You are meant to be together. Why don't you get married in six months?" I took that advice and proposed to her that day!

> Proverbs 15:22 (GNT)
> Get all the advice you can, and you will succeed;
> without it you will fail.

> *Proverbs 12:15 (NLT)*
> Fools think their own way is right,
> but the wise listen to others.

One of my favorite verses about asking for counsel is Proverbs 11:14. Here is how I have memorized the reference for this verse. How many people does it take to make a "multitude?" Let's say somewhere between 11 and 14 people... therefore, Proverbs 11:14.

> *Proverbs 11:14 (NKJV)*
> Where there is no counsel, the people fall;
> But in the multitude of counselors there is safety.

There is safety and wisdom in getting counsel from the right people. When we face important decisions, we should seek advice from key voices in our lives, including our spouse, parents, and pastors.

We should also seek out people who are older than we are and ask for their wisdom and perspective. The Bible says that people with gray hair have extra wisdom. I've seen the truth of that in my own life—I can give better advice now because I know of all the mistakes I have made! If I could do things over again, I would make wiser choices.

Proverbs 20:29 (NLT)
The glory of the young is their strength;
the gray hair of experience is the splendor of the old.

I remember approaching an older church member once when I was single and thinking about dating and marriage. I asked him, "What is your best advice in finding a partner?"

He replied with something so profound, "Fifty years is a long time to be married to the wrong person."

I never forgot that. When I started dating Connie, I wondered if I could put up with her favorite "elephant jokes" for fifty years.

Some people only ask for counsel from those they know will agree with what they already want to do. That isn't very helpful or safe, though. It is best to ask people who you know will pray about it and give you their honest, wise opinion without fear of what you might think.

One time a young man came to me asking for counsel about a job opportunity in another city far away. He was very excited, and he told me he could make more money at this job, and it would have many other benefits. He went on and on. Finally, after about an hour, he asked me what I thought.

I answered, "Well, my first comment is this. You've talked a long time about the decision, but I never once heard you say that you prayed about it, or that you prayed with your wife about it, or that you felt God leading you. If you want my opinion, I don't think you should go based on that fact alone. The more you spoke about it, the more I felt that you could be missing God's will."

He got a bit offended by that. I said, "You are an adult. You can do what you want. But you asked my opinion, so I'm giving it to you."

He went ahead and moved to the other city. About six months later, he moved back home. The offer was not as good as he thought. He came to me and said, "Brian, I should have taken your advice and prayed about it more. I lost six months of my time and about $10,000."

I remember many years ago, a guest speaker in our church prophesied over me. He had insight from God for my life when I was just eighteen. Everything he said over me has been fulfilled in the forty-six years since then. He became a friend and mentor who often gave me divine guidance.

I am grateful for the many people God has used to guide me over the years through the gift of prophecy and for the life-changing, divine words they gave me. I would not be where I am today if it weren't for those individuals and their wise counsel.

> **PUT IT INTO PRACTICE:** *Make a list of three wise people you trust to give you godly counsel. Message one of them, and invite them out for lunch or coffee this week. Talk, then listen. Ask questions and pay attention to their answers. Pray together with them. Often people like this will pray and think about the conversation later, then get back to you with their advice.*

9. Start Over Again (If You Need To)

Have you made mistakes? Who *hasn't* made mistakes?

Does God still have a great future for you? Can you still accomplish His will for your life? *Yes!*

In the Bible, God forgave and used many imperfect people who did things wrong. King David made some serious mistakes, but when he sincerely returned to God and repented, God forgave him. David was known as a man after God's own heart.

Isaiah 43:18, 19 (NJKV)

Do not remember the former things, nor consider the things of

> old. Behold, I will do a new thing, now it shall spring forth; shall you not know it? I will even make a road in the wilderness and rivers in the desert.

I remember one person who told me, "I have made so many mistakes and messed up for so many years. I am going to live for God with so much zeal that I catch up on the years that I lost."

> **PUT IT INTO PRACTICE:** *Forget the past. Don't even consider it. Don't let it occupy one second of your mind anymore! Start over now. Draw near to God and ask Him what He wants you to do for Him. Focus on the future. Focus on Jesus.*
>
> *Claim the promises in this encouraging portion of scripture about how God can help you get out of a cold winter season and back into a spring growth season for your life.*
>
> *Song of Solomon 2:11, 12 (NKJV)*
> *Look, the winter is past, and the rains are over and gone. The flowers are springing up, the season of singing birds has come, and the cooing of turtledoves fills the air.*
>
> *"Nobody is a total failure if he dares to try to do something worthwhile."*
> *—Robert Schuller*

16. EMPOWERING POTENTIAL

HAVE YOU EVER SEEN A 930-POUND PUMPKIN? Pumpkins in Canada ripen every October. The average pumpkin size sold in grocery stores is around 20 pounds. This picture illustrates the vast difference in size between a 20-pound fruit and a 930-pound fruit! Just imagine the incredible, flourishing plant that produced such an enormous pumpkin.

Giant 930-lb pumpkin grown by local farmers in Canada.

Psalm 92:12-14 (NKJV)
The righteous shall flourish like a palm tree,
He shall grow like a cedar in Lebanon.
Those who are planted in the house of the Lord
Shall flourish in the courts of our God.
They shall still bear fruit in old age;
They shall be fresh and flourishing.

The word flourish is mentioned three times in Psalm 92, and it means "to come to peak performance, to the best potential possible; to grow in a healthy or vigorous way; to develop rapidly and successfully; to be working at the height of one's career."

I believe that to flourish, we must be "planted" in a church. There are so many great benefits to being part of a strong local church. Connie and I have attended the same church since 1978, and we have seen how vital being planted in a church has been in guiding us into our life purpose. We have had the same pastors, Mel and Heather Mullen, the entire time. Now their son, Jachin, and his wife Rebecca are the lead pastors of Home Church worldwide.

At Home Church, we have five core values that outline what we feel the Lord has asked us to do. Everything we do as a church should be consistent with these values. Pastor Mel Mullen, the founder of Home Church, in his book, *Experience Jesus and His Church*, explained these five critical values that we use as foundations in all of our international church locations. These same values can guide you to another level of your calling.

1. Engaging the culture
2. Authentic relationships
3. Empowering potential
4. Driven by compassion
5. For all generations, ages, and people groups

The most important thing we do is lead everyone we can to connect with Jesus. After His resurrection, He told 500 followers to "Go and make disciples!" (Matthew 28:19 NLT). If Jesus were on the earth talking to His followers today, He would say the same thing. He has a plan for this world and for every person's eternal destiny. He wants us to tell others. He wants us to share our testimonies, which are our stories of how we connected with Jesus. This is the first step that will help all of us on the road to our calling. *The number one reason you and I are on this planet is to tell people about Jesus.*

Our Home Church mission statement sums this up: "Everyone needs Jesus and everyone needs a home."

Notice that one of the core values is "driven by compassion." Home of Hope is not an independent humanitarian organization, but rather the compassion arm of our church. I believe every person or church that helps the poor will be blessed. We are blessed to be a blessing.

I believe Jesus is the answer to the many problems I have referred to in this book. As people learn and follow Biblical principles, they can find hope and help. The local church is the next step to enable people to find practical solutions.

All of the children we help through Home of Hope are invited to church to learn more about Jesus. One of my favorite goals for HOH is helping 5,000 *new* children every year. To bring lasting change in a child's life, we tell them about Jesus immediately. Almost all children say a prayer to ask Jesus into their lives, and it is so fulfilling to know that the new children we help every year are going to heaven!

Earlier, I referred to the story of the Good Samaritan (Luke 10:25-37), in which a person from Samaria noticed someone hurt and lying in a ditch. He went out of his way to do everything possible to help the wounded man. He put him on his donkey, took him to the nearest inn, and paid the bill while the man recovered. We all need to be like the Good Samaritan and follow his example. The church, in my opinion, is the inn where people can get the necessary help to get back on their feet. The church is called to care for, love, and support people in need.

As of the writing of this book, Home Church is in over 120 locations in 13 nations! We have laid the foundation to plant an average of one church every week this coming year, including church plants in three new countries.

Empowering Future Champions

I want to empower people to fulfill what God has called them to do. Our purpose is not to have people around us who make us look good or serve us. It is about using who we are to bring the potential out of every life we can. We should all desire to have a servant's heart and to help others succeed.

This Bible verse has been a favorite of mine for many years. It motivates me to keep going and do as much as I can with God's help.

> *Daniel 11:32b (NKJV)*
> ...but the people who know their God shall be strong and carry out great exploits.

Throughout this book, I have shared testimonies of many of our international HOH team members who have risen up and done great things. They are champions! They are people who have done exploits, and I am so proud of them.

The word exploits, as a noun, is a powerful word in the Bible. It means "a notable, memorable, or heroic act." All of us want to do something that will make a difference. Accomplishing exploits starts with knowing God! Get closer to God and receive His strength. I love the NASB 1995 translation of the same verse: "But the people who know their God will display strength and take action."

Knowing God makes us stronger, and being stronger leads us to make a difference. If you or someone you know is not actively helping others, the answer is to draw closer to God. He has a part for everyone to play in His master plan, and there is great fulfillment when we serve in church or through church ministries. When I teach, I often quote this verse:

> *James 2:17 (NIV)*
> In the same way, faith by itself, if it is not accompanied by action, is dead.

For me, this verse means we must have an action plan. I have met many Christians who are praying hard and waiting for something to happen, but they don't take any tangible steps to discover and enter into their calling. Remember, knowing God leads to *obeying* God, and that always involves *action*. I believe God will give us an action plan as a key part of the miracle He wants to do through us. As we act, the miracle happens, and the exploits take place.

We usually don't know the full extent of that plan initially, and we will need to learn and grow along the way. Therefore, to carry out God's plan and reach our full potential, we must embrace two essential principles: training and pruning. Let's look at these one at a time.

Training Is Key

I have patterned a lot of what I do in helping others reach their potential after how Paul the apostle mentored his best and most loyal team member, Timothy.

2 Timothy 2:1-2 (NLT)

> Timothy, my dear son, be strong through the grace that God gives you in Christ Jesus. You have heard me teach things that have been confirmed by many reliable witnesses. Now teach these truths to other trustworthy people who will be able to pass them on to others.

There was a divine connection and love between Paul and Timothy. It is so fulfilling when God sovereignly connects me with new team members around the world. We often say we are "friends for life," and we have named some of our conferences "Friendships for Life."

I have developed a weekly routine of pouring my life into key leaders. I meet with them online for mentoring, coaching, friendship, and prayer. Often, I feel free to share my struggles and challenges with them, and they are so supportive.

For example, I mentioned that I meet with our national leaders online every week. We discuss what we feel God is saying to us and talk about how to improve our projects to reach more people and to move forward together in unity. Our leaders continue to grow through this process and some have become champions. Training is hard work! We are starting many more churches over the coming years, and our projects are expanding in every nation we are working in. We train our overseers to grow their team of wonderful people who they train and lead as well. Some of our leaders used to be discouraged with only a few people, but now they are leading many successful people. And the best is yet to come—as they are empowered to reach their potential, they do the same for their own teams and many others.

Paul trained Timothy and then challenged him to pass it on to others who are faithful. Pastor Jachin uses the word "swivel" as an illustration of this concept. He explained it by sitting in an office chair that swivels. When he gives important teaching or direction to us in Canada, we receive it from him, then we (figuratively) spin 180 degrees in our chairs and pass the instruction on to those we work with. They, in turn, swivel it to their teams around the world.

Pastor Fidele is another example of someone who has been transformed by training and is accomplishing incredible things. He has been a faithful leader in Rwanda for over thirteen years. He felt God led him to join us, and one of our first comments to him was that we promised no financial assistance at all. He has chosen to live by faith and trust in God as his provider. Marvelous miracles began to happen because the Holy Spirit led him and because of the consistent training that came from our "One Church" vision in Canada. We don't teach Canadian customs, but we believe that what God has given us is a working model to plant churches and expand the Home of Hope projects in any country and culture of the world. That is why our vision is called One Church.

My schedule is usually full of meetings with overseers from various countries. We have many weekly online international chats with Home Church leaders around the world. We also go on frequent trips to see all of our leaders and teach and train them onsite, as well as hosting other training times for our pastors and HOH leaders around the world. Sometimes we need to talk about adjustments and changes that must happen; other times we simply deepen the friendship and encourage each other in the Lord. Training is so important for all of us to go to another level of flourishing.

Training is not a one-time thing. It lasts our whole lives because we can always grow and learn, especially as we step into new areas of our calling. Whether you are receiving training, giving training, or some of both, take advantage of the power of teaching to unlock potential.

Permission to Prune

Teaching and training are exciting words. Pruning... not so much. And yet, it is an essential and ultimately liberating principle for bearing much fruit.

John 15 explains how pruning plants enables them to produce more fruit. In the same way, pruning in our lives can be painful, but it is essential to growing more fruit. I have used the principle of pruning many times in my teaching and one-on-one mentoring. God is glorified when we bear much fruit. That is the goal of pruning.

> *John 15:1-8 (NLT)*
> I am the true grapevine, and my Father is the gardener. He cuts off every branch of mine that doesn't produce fruit, and he prunes the branches that do bear fruit so they will produce even more. You have already been pruned and purified by the message I have given you. Remain in me, and I will remain in you. For a branch cannot produce fruit if it is severed from the vine, and you cannot be fruitful unless you remain in me.
>
> Yes, I am the vine; you are the branches. Those who remain in me, and I in them, will produce much fruit. For apart from me you can do nothing. Anyone who does not remain in me is thrown away like a useless branch and withers. Such branches are gathered into a pile to be burned. But if you remain in me and my words remain in you, you may ask for anything you want, and it will be granted! When you produce much fruit, you are my true disciples. This brings great glory to my Father.

It is exciting to see people start to produce fruit and see the joy on their faces. But when they go through times of pruning, they are usually not so happy about it. We often don't see the reason for pruning at the moment.

Growing up on the farm, I watched my mother prune her tomato plants. She would cut off perfect green branches, and it was such a puzzle to me. Often, the tomato plant would start so green and full, but it would look thinned out and kind of ugly after she was done with it. She would say, "I only leave the branches that have a bud on them. That bud is the start of fruit that will grow on that branch someday." Days or weeks later, though, the plant would be full of big, bright red tomatoes that I enjoyed picking and eating.

A good sentence to say to people you feel could help develop your potential is this: "If you ever see anything that would hinder me from becoming more fruitful for God, please tell me."

As I think back over the people I have pastored for over forty years, it is easy to see who became fruitful and who refused the pruning of God and the pruning of others who God put in their lives. It is sad to see great potential not realized.

Never forget how important you are. Your story matters. You *must* have others who can train, mentor, coach, and cheer you on to reach your full potential. Both training and pruning are essential to take you where you are capable of going.

- I would never be where I am at today without someone praying over me and saying, "Brian, I think God wants you to go to Rwanda and plant churches and help orphans."

- Lynzee was very shy and had never stood on stage. She overcame her fears and influenced hundreds of people with her testimony.

- George was on his way to becoming an engineer, but then someone prayed over him and encouraged him to rescue babies someday. He chose to follow his heart, and he has saved hundreds of babies. He has never regretted the choice he made.

- Andrew believed in Vishwa, whose mother had told him that he was too ugly, and helped him rebuild his life to fulfill his destiny.

We are called to do great things in Jesus. He doesn't want us to be normal, average pumpkin plants, but rather growing, flourishing plants that bring forth amazing fruit. Being able to bless people on this level is the thrill of advancing in our calling.

Do you want to flourish and achieve all that God has for you? Do you want to become the person you were created to be?

Never forget: you are **Meant 4 More!**

17. WE'RE NOT STOPPING NOW

I don't know all that God has in store for Home of Hope, but our present goal is to continue helping 5,000 new children every year. As generous people give donations, we are able to help more and more children.

God gave me a promise that has carried me since the start of HOH. It has been one of the biggest keys of financial provision in my life and for our family.

> *Proverbs 28:27* (*NASB*)
> One who gives to the poor will never lack anything, but one who shuts his eyes will have many curses.

Isn't that a fantastic promise? When I read that verse in the Bible as HOH started, it came alive to me. It was as if God was telling me, "Brian, if you take care of the poor, I will take care of you!" I knew at that moment that I was not to take one cent of any donation people gave to the poor for myself.

I remember one time when our personal finances were very tight, and Connie said, "Brian, the Bible says that a cow that treads out the crop is allowed to eat some of the grain. It is scriptural for you to receive some salary from HOH." She was referring to 1 Corinthians 9:9-11, which talks about ministers being given financial support for their work.

I replied, "I feel like God doesn't want me to be paid from any donation for the poor. But let's pray about it and talk in a week."

Two days later, I received a phone call from a complete stranger. He said, "Are you Brian Thomson, the one who is helping babies who are thrown away in Kenya?"

I said, "Yes."

He asked if he and his wife could take us out for lunch. As we were eating together, they asked many questions about what we were doing and what we felt called by God to do. They loved hearing about the rescued babies and kept asking me to tell more stories. As I shared about the children, I could not hold back my tears. Connie had to finish some of the stories for me.

Then they started asking us some personal questions, including about how I was paid. I explained that our local church gives us a sponsorship every month, and the rest comes from honorariums when we speak in churches. They asked if I received any money from Home of Hope donations.

I said, "Not a penny."

They replied, "We want to give a gift to what you are doing, but is it okay if it goes to you personally? If you don't have your needs met, what will happen to this great work of helping so many children?"

As lunch was wrapping up, they pulled out a sealed envelope and gave it to us. Afterward, we thanked them and said goodbye.

We opened the envelope together and were shocked to see that it was enough money to pay the remaining part of my monthly salary and some money to help cover travel expenses for my upcoming trips for an entire year! Connie looked at me, shook her head, and we just smiled at each other. God is so good. Within a couple of days of our discussion about finances, God had confirmed to me that I should not receive money as the founder and director of Home of Hope, but instead I was to trust in Him to provide for my salary and travel expenses.

We are so thankful for the sponsors who have given generously to HOH children and projects, but I am also grateful for those who have given to me personally. This has helped the administration fees of HOH stay so low.

Worry Less, Trust More

Another Bible passage that has given me faith for God's supply is Matthew 6:25-33. The Bible says that God knows all of our needs before we even ask Him. God feeds the birds, and we are *far more valuable* to Him than birds. God promises that He will take care of us and provide food for us, and we are not to live in worry. The Bible also says that He loves us more than the beautiful flowers. He promises to give us what we need for clothes as well as what we need to drink.

This promise is conditional, though. *If* we seek first God's Kingdom and His righteousness, we may claim these promises. Read this portion of scripture slowly and prayerfully. If you have financial needs, I hope it will encourage you and be part of a breakthrough for you.

> *Matthew 6:25-33 (NLT)*
> That is why I tell you not to worry about everyday life—whether you have enough food and drink, or enough clothes to wear. Isn't life more than food, and your body more than clothing? Look at the birds. They don't plant or harvest or store food in barns, for your heavenly Father feeds them. And aren't you far more valuable to him than they are? Can all your worries add a single moment to your life?
>
> And why worry about your clothing? Look at the lilies of the field and how they grow. They don't work or make their clothing, yet Solomon in all his glory was not dressed as beautifully as they

> are. And if God cares so wonderfully for wildflowers that are here today and thrown into the fire tomorrow, he will certainly care for you. Why do you have so little faith?
>
> So don't worry about these things, saying, 'What will we eat? What will we drink? What will we wear?' These things dominate the thoughts of unbelievers, but your heavenly Father already knows all your needs. Seek the Kingdom of God above all else, and live righteously, and he will give you everything you need.

That last verse is so good! If we seek *His* Kingdom above all else, and He will give us *everything* we need. Let's focus our attention on what God wants us to do today and in the future. Put Him first every day by reading the Bible and praying to Him. Put Him first every week by going to your local church to worship Him.

And, put Him first in your finances by bringing the first part of your income to the local church. The Bible talks about tithes and offerings. We are blessed when we give a tithe of our income to the local church, but we can also give generous offerings to help the poor and serve people in need.

We have received countless testimonies from people who began to give toward HOH projects, and then *miracles started happening for them*. We have also had many people tell us they had a miraculous pregnancy after they began sponsoring a child. Isn't that astounding? While we do not give to get, we experience the reality of God's goodness when we follow God's ways.

Giving doesn't guarantee us a specific miracle, but it does ensure we will be benefactors of God's loving care. I'm not telling you these things to manipulate you for a donation, nor do I promise a particular miracle. I'm simply sharing testimonies of what God has done for me and for others who have been generous with the resources He has given us. After all, the Bible is full of promises that when we help orphans, the fatherless, and the poor, God will take care of us.

Financial Integrity

One of my catchphrases is, "It's more fun with money." When a need is brought to our attention, it is exciting to be able to say that we have the money to cover the need. As more money comes in, we can help more children and meet more needs. I know this seems obvious, but we promise that money designated toward a specific Home of Hope project will be used for that project until all expenses are covered.

As more money comes in for shoes, more children will get shoes! As more money comes in for food, more children will be served by our feeding programs. The same goes for health cards, school tuition, animal projects, and microloans. Our HOH international team provides transparency through receipts, pictures, and reports demonstrating that all funds are spent with integrity.

Most transactions are entirely cashless from start to finish. We can wire money or transfer it electronically for spending nearly anywhere in the world now. We do our best to give updates on projects and sponsored children every six months, and we choose to have our financial statements audited on an annual basis.

There Is Always Another Chapter

In those early days of helping children, I cried a lot because God's love was operating upon my heart. Why do I still cry fourteen years later? I've teared up when someone sacrificially gave $5, or a retired person apologizes that she can only afford to give $20 a month. I've cried often when I receive gripping pictures from an international HOH team member who needs financial aid for a desperate child.

One time, we heard about a child who was malnourished and about to die, and we sent money as fast as possible, but it was too late. The child died before the money arrived. It broke our hearts. Since then, sponsors have helped create an emergency rescue fund that is always ready to save children who need immediate help.

None of this would have been possible without God moving on people's hearts. It wouldn't have happened if God hadn't shown me that all of us—me, the children and families we serve, and *you*—are **Meant 4 More**.

I have invested many tears into writing this book—retelling and reliving the stories that have changed my life. I hope it has ignited your passion for doing what you are meant to do in this life. Don't wait!

Maybe you want to get on your knees as I did and ask God what the next chapter of your life is. He rarely reveals the whole story, but He *will* tell you the next chapter. As He did with Abraham, God reveals our steps gradually, one at a time.

It started with 4 children for me. We are not stopping with 10,000, nor with 5,000 new children every year. I will continue to do everything I can to help children for the rest of my life. I am experiencing my destiny, and I am fulfilled in my purpose. I'll say it one last time: *It's for the children!*

HOW TO GET INVOLVED

CONTACT US

Home of Hope: www.homeofhope.ca
Home Church: www.myhomechurch.ca
Home Church Bible College: www.homechurchbiblecollege.com

Email: info@homeofhope.ca
Phone: +1-403-343-6570 Extension 6
Mailing address: 37557 Highway 2A
Red Deer County, Alberta, Canada T4E1S2

Registration #11909 1031 RR0001

AVAILABLE ON OUR WEBSITE

- Children waiting for monthly sponsorship
- How to sign up for a waiting list to sponsor and name a baby
- How to apply for a Home of Hope Discovery trip
- Present needs and the emergency fund
- How to sponsor members of our growing staff
- Information on Brian and how to contribute to his work

We also have hundreds of pictures, stories, and videos on our social media posts, including countless examples illustrating the seven ways we help children.

PROJECT VS. ADMINISTRATION COSTS

We keep our administration costs as low as possible. Only 10% of donations is allocated for the Canadian HOH office operating expenses and 3.5% for financial management, tax receipting, and yearly audit costs through Home Church. This means 86.5% of donations go toward designated projects, and 13.5% goes to administration. We issue tax receipts for all gifts over $15.00.

TO CONTACT BRIAN THOMSON

Website: www.brianthomson.com
Email: brian.thomson@myhomechurch.ca
Facebook: www.facebook.com/brianwthomson
Join www.facebook.com/groups/adventureswithbrian to follow my trip adventures.

Scan the QR code below or visit linktr.ee/meant4morebook to access additional video, social media, and websites highlighting Home of Hope projects.

SPECIAL THANKS

I wrote a book a long time ago, and I honestly dreaded writing another one. Within the span of five days, however, many friends and family encouraged me to write my story. I couldn't travel, so I worked very hard while in lockdown from COVID-19. I am so glad I did!

I poured so many hours and tears into writing this book because I wanted to share my story and the stories of the children in order to inspire *you*. You, too, can make a difference.

Thank you to everyone who has ever given to Home of Hope, whether it was $1 to feed a child, or a gift to me personally, or any other form of support. You are invaluable, and you have made a difference.

Thank you, Pastors Jachin and Rebecca Mullen, lead pastors of Home Church. It is an honor to be part of such a great team. Your love for Jesus and your all-in, dedicated attitude is wonderful. We are 100% behind you and with you, and the best days are ahead.

Our founding pastors, Mel and Heather, have been our pastors for over forty years. We always say that our goal is to be like Billy Graham, who had some of his team with him for over sixty years. Thank you for your love and counsel to Connie and me. We have enjoyed working with you both for all these years.

Thank you to the church legal board, which has been actively involved in giving wisdom and direction to our international projects.

Thank you to my fantastic wife, Connie, who has believed in me and supported me through all the transitions and changes. She is constantly pruning me to make me a better person. She loves her children and grandchildren and is doing all she can to help them discover how they are **Meant 4 More**. She also worked very hard on editing and sculpting this book. I think she needs to write a book soon.

Thank you to our daughter Karissa for the initial vision to put this book together. She worked hard at gathering stories and pictures, compiling, and proofreading, which requires a lot of work and collaboration!

As I mentioned in the book, I am thankful for all of our children and their spouses for being so active with Home of Hope and what God has called me to do. We have always been not just family, but close friends who are serving God together. This is truly a family ministry.

Thank you to our Home Church international overseers and Home of Hope team members in Rwanda, Kenya, Congo, Malawi, and India.

Special thanks to Dan Peters, Dan Wiebe, Florence Thomson, and Lynzee Berreth who are so important as my advisory team.

Thank you to all the contributors who shared their stories to illustrate how God is using Home of Hope to change lives.

Thank you, Mark Weber, for bringing your twenty-two years of expertise in editing! You have a great heart to donate your time for the cause of this book.

Thank you, Justin Jaquith, for doing such a fantastic job professionally editing this book. You took my tricky and sometimes confusing stories and wording and made them flow so beautifully. I couldn't have done this project without you.

Thank you again to the Hoovers who passed on the torch of Home of Hope India to us.

Thank you, Matthew Barnett, from the LA Dream Center, for allowing us to use the name Dream Centre.

Thank you, Jesus, my greatest hero and Savior. Please give me the opportunity to continue to serve for many years to come. I know I am **Meant 4 (Even) More.**

MEET THE AUTHOR

Brian and Connie Thomson have been on staff with Home Church since 1979, first serving with Pastors Mel and Heather Mullen (the founding pastors) and now with Lead Pastors Jachin and Becca Mullen. They served as youth pastors, then Bible college directors and associate pastors. Brian started traveling in full-time evangelism ministry in 1995. He has his doctorate in practical ministry.

Brian now helps gives oversight to many of the 120 Home Church locations in 13 different countries as the International Director. He serves as the Director of Home of Hope, the compassion-based outreach arm of Home Church, which is helping thousands of vulnerable children in many countries and regions. Connie is part of the HOH team in the national office and often travels with Brian.

Home of Hope Rwanda started in December 2006, when Brian went to Rwanda to investigate the needs of orphans and widows. Rwanda had one of the greatest needs for orphan aid in the world at the time due to the 1994 genocide and the HIV/AIDS epidemic. The nation's needs gripped him, and Brian became the founder and director of Home of Hope Rwanda. Home of Hope has now spread to many other countries, including Kenya, DR Congo, Malawi, and India.

Brian and his wife, Connie, both grew up on farms in Central Alberta, Canada. They attended the same small country school. After they became Christians at age sixteen, their lives began to head in the same direction. They have been happily married since 1979 and have been blessed with two sons, two daughters, two daughters-in-law, two sons-in-law, and now thirteen delightful grandchildren.